LAKE SUPERIOR FLAVORS

LAKE SUPERIOR FLAVORS

A FIELD GUIDE TO FOOD AND DRINK
ALONG THE CIRCLE TOUR

JAMES NORTON

PHOTOGRAPHY *by* BECCA DILLEY

University of Minnesota Press
Minneapolis · London

The University of Minnesota Press gratefully acknowledges the generous assistance provided for the publication of this book by the Hamilton P. Traub University Press Fund.

Published by the University of Minnesota Press
111 Third Avenue South, Suite 290
Minneapolis, MN 55401-2520
http://www.upress.umn.edu

Design and production by Mighty Media, Inc.
Interior and text design by Chris Long

ISBN 978-0-8166-7544-9
A Cataloging-in-Publication record for this book is available from the Library of Congress.

Printed in Canada on acid-free paper

The University of Minnesota is an equal-opportunity educator and employer.

20 19 18 17 16 15 14   10 9 8 7 6 5 4 3 2 1

To my grandfather, James L. Norton, who loved the lake

CONTENTS

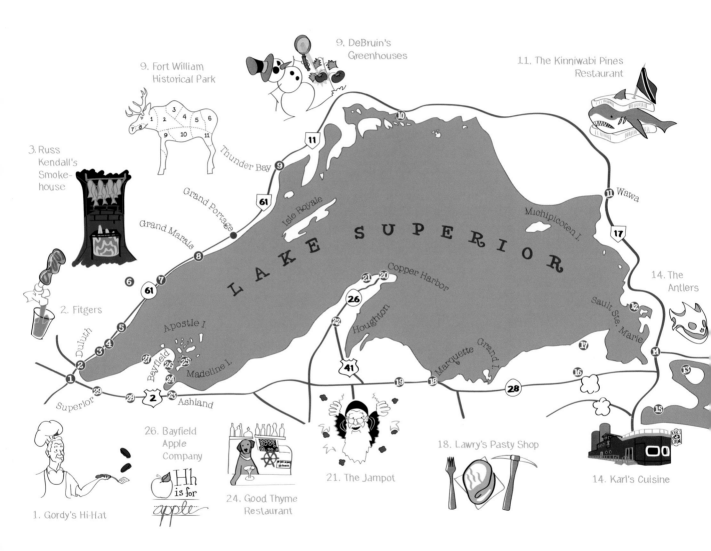

9. Fort William
Historical Park

9. DeBruin's
Greenhouses

11. The Kinniwabi Pines
Restaurant

3. Russ
Kendall's
Smoke-
house

Thunder Bay

Grand Portage

Grand Marais

Wawa

Michipicoten I.

L A K E   S U P E R I O R

Isle Royale

2. Fitgers

Duluth

Apostle I.

Bayfield

Madeline I.

Copper Harbor

Houghton

Grand I.

Marquette

Sault Ste. Marie

14. The
Antlers

41

Superior

Ashland

2

19

18

28

16

15

13

14

26. Bayfield
Apple
Company

Hh
is for
apple

24. Good Thyme
Restaurant

21. The Jampot

18. Lawry's Pasty Shop

14. Karl's Cuisine

1. Gordy's Hi-Hat

The Circle Tour of Lake Superior.

MINNESOTA

1. **Cloquet**
   Gordy's Hi-Hat

2. **Duluth**
   Northern Waters
     Smokehaus
   Fitger's Brewhouse
   Duluth Coffee
     Company
   JJ Astor Restaurant
     and Lounge
   Tycoons, the Zenith
     Alehouse
   Lake Superior
     Brewing
   New Scenic Café

3. **Knife River**
   Russ Kendall's
     Smokehouse
   Borealis Fermentery

4. **Two Harbors**
   Vanilla Bean Café

5. **Castle Danger**
   Rustic Inn Café

6. **Finland**
   Round River Farm

7. **Schroeder**
   Satellite's Country
     Inn

8. **Grand Marais**
   Angry Trout Café
   Dockside Fish
     Market
   The Naniboujou
     Lodge
   The World's Best
     Donuts

CANADA

9. **Thunder Bay**
   Harri Bakery
   The Fish Shop
   DeBruin's
     Greenhouses
   Northern Unique
   The Growing Season
     Juice Collective
   Boreal Forest Teas
   Bears' Bees and
     Honey
   Belluz Farms
   Ojibwa Food
     Traditions
   Thunder Oak Cheese
     Farm
   Hoito
   Thunder Bay
     Country Market
   Kangas Sauna and
     Restaurant
   The Beer Store
   The Persian Man
   Caribou Restaurant
     and Wine Bar

10. **Rossport**
    Serendipity Gardens
      Café

11. **Wawa**
    The Kinniwabi Pines
      Restaurant
    Young's General
      Store

12. **Batchawana Bay**
    Salzburger Hof

13. **St. Joseph Island**
    Gilbertson's Pancake
      House
    Harmony Tea Room

MICHIGAN

14. **Sault Ste. Marie**
    Karl's Cuisine
    Goetz's Lockview
      Restaurant
    The Antlers

15. **St. Ignace**
    Clyde's

16. **Newberry**
    North Star Brick
      Oven Bakery

17. **Paradise**
    Tahquamenon Falls
      Brewery and Pub

18. **Marquette**
    Casa Calabria
    Elizabeth's Chop
      House
    Lawry's Pasty Shop
    The North Star
      Lounge

19. **Ishpeming**
    Ralph's Italian Deli

20. **Copper Harbor**
    Harbor Haus

21. **Eagle Harbor**
    The Jampot Bakery

22. **Houghton**
    Suomi Home Bakery
      and Restaurant
    Keweenaw Brewing
      Company

WISCONSIN

23. **Ashland**
    Maslowski Beach
    South Shore
      Brewery
    Deep Water Grille

24. **Washburn**
    Good Thyme
      Restaurant

25. **Madeline Island**
    Tom's Burned Down
      Café

26. **Bayfield**
    Bayfield Apple
      Company
    Rittenhouse Inn
    Judy's Gourmet
      Garage
    Bodin Fisheries and
      Seafood Market

27. **Herbster**
    Sassy Nanny
      Farmstead Cheese

28. **Iron River**
    White Winter
      Winery

29. **Superior**
    Thirsty Pagan
      Brewing
    Anchor Bar

Lakeside dining along Superior's shores.

INTRODUCTION

THERE IS ALWAYS A TEMPTATION to tell the story of Lake Superior using facts and figures. The lake has 31,700 square miles of surface area, for example. It takes nearly two hundred years for the water in the lake to turn over completely. (For comparison's sake: Lake Erie, the smallest Great Lake by volume, turns over every two and a half years.) Some of the rock near the lake goes back to the creation of the earth as we know it—it's 2.7 billion years old, give or take a century or two. Pick up any book about Superior, and there's a good chance it starts along these lines, with a recitation of numbers.

This sort of reaction—a retreat into statistics—is a common human response to the grandeur of nature. When we're confronted with something so big that we can't really understand it, we grasp for measurements, for comfort. It's a way to reconcile our abstract understanding that Lake Superior is "big" with the concrete reality of standing on the shore of an inland sea that is very much its own place, and feels as though it has its own time, too—measured more by glaciers, weather patterns, and migrations than by days, months, and years.

More than anything, Lake Superior is still a wild place, a stark, rocky landscape facing a vast stretch of cold water. With its famously long and brutal winters and consequently short growing season, it's a minor wonder that the Lake Superior region was settled at all. But where there is a place—even a place as often forbidding as Lake Superior—there is great food to be had. And where there is food, there is a story.

This book is dedicated to telling the stories of Lake Superior's food culture: tasting the food and drink and talking to the people who catch, cook, forage, brew, bake, and otherwise produce it, with special emphasis on the connection between the land, the water, and the table.

We based this book on numerous trips to the lake to visit with its people and taste its food, including two full, clockwise circle tours from Duluth to Superior, the long way around. While we've presented the book as a single sweep around the lake's perimeter, bear in mind that the story we tell is actually informed by a number of different visits and other supporting research.

The book is broken into four main sections, corresponding to the four major parts of the lake best known by travelers and locals alike. Each has its own character, and whenever possible, we do our best to explore the wrinkles that divide the various regions of Superior as well as the gastronomic aspects that unite them. We'll travel from the once tycoon-studded North Shore to the stark and wild Canadian part of the lake, with a marvelous and productive stop in the regenerating city of Thunder Bay, to the genially rustic Upper Peninsula and, finally, to the laid-back and civilized environs of the South Shore's alphabet cities: Ashland, Bayfield, and Cornucopia.

We intend that this book serve half as a guide—many of our trips are easily recreatable and highly recommended—and half as a journal of our voyages that tells a broader story about food and drink on the shores of the lake. We hope that it will serve, in equal parts, as fuel for the imagination and a practical handbook to how best to eat one's way around the lake.

Some of the food we ate was profoundly humble—burgers and pizza, diner fare and doughnuts. By the time you've finished this book, you will have joined us for beer in Superior and Persians (frosted doughnuts) in Thunder Bay, and will understand the soulful sophistication and deep thought that goes into something like the herring roe appetizer at the Angry Trout in Grand Marais and the lobsteresque taste of "beer blanc" whitefish at the South Shore Brewery in Ashland.

Just as important as the food are the fascinating people behind it. In short, Lake Superior favors the creative, the passionate, and the brave: the lazy move somewhere warmer and easier. When we set out on our trips around the lake, we didn't know whom we would meet, or what we would learn. On the Keweenaw Peninsula, we met jam-making monks who work in the forest far from the troubles of the modern world.

We met a goatherd who walks with his flock into the woods of northern Wisconsin, sipping a cocktail as he takes in the night air. And we met many more people along the way: a brewer working in the shadows of an ancient waterfall, a boreal forest herbal forager who sells teas harvested from the northern woods, a Trinidadian family serving shark along the side of the Trans-Canada highway, and a fisherman-scholar who spends his shore time handcrafting Norwegian musical instruments.

Our story is premised on the idea that food "local" to Lake Superior exists and that it can be tasted, described, and enjoyed. But the question as to what makes food "local" is an open one. Is coffee grown in South America, shipped to a major trans-shipment warehouse in the United States, broken down into small parcels, shipped to Duluth, and then roasted in a resident's outbuilding "local coffee"? Is local food really Trinidadian-style shark caught off the coast of Venezuela and delivered by food service company truck to the Canadian shore of Lake Superior, where it is then cooked and served with love and care according to a family recipe? Or must local food completely embrace the *terroir*—the sense of place imparted by weather, mineralogy, other living things, and a host of other factors—of where it's from?

As much as possible, we've explored food that echoes the terroir of Lake Superior, ranging from honey made by bees that feed on local flowers, to fish from the lake smoked with local wood, to beer brewed with local hops and local water. But as we traveled around Lake Superior, we turned an inclusive eye on the region's offerings. That shark didn't come from Wawa, but the fact that it's served there and the story of how it got there help paint the picture of how people eat and why they choose to settle on the lake's shore. And when we write about the pasties of Michigan's Upper Peninsula, we're aware that they tell not just the story of Michigan mining culture but also of Cornwall, and that while all their component ingredients might not be from nearby farms and ranches, eating a pasty is a cultural statement for those who live in the UP.

All this is to say that "local" food is in the eye of the beholder. It's probably not Tim Hortons, unless by local you mean "North America." And it's probably not Kraft singles purchased at a gas station. But beyond that, we're allowing our readers the liberty of deciding what makes local food local, and giving you as much information as we can so that you can make up your mind as you travel with us along the shores of Lake Superior. ⬦

MINNESOTA'S NORTH SHORE

FROM SMOKED TROUT TO BIG BOAT STOUT

If any area of Minnesota answers to nineteenth-century notions of the sublime, it is the North Shore of Lake Superior . . . it could as well be an ocean.

Paul Clifford Larson, *A Place at the Lake*

MINNESOTA'S NORTH SHORE AT A GLANCE

Although there are outposts to the north and west of Minnesota's North Shore, travelers get the distinct sensation that they are sliding along an increasingly thin knife's edge of civilization as they pass through Duluth and head toward the Canadian border. At a combined population of 279,771 (according to the 2010 census), the Duluth–Superior metropolitan area is the biggest on the lake, but that's a drop in the bucket compared to the Twin Cities, which clocks in at more than 3 million people. Travel north, and the numbers drop quickly: 3,745 in Two Harbors, 1,351 in Grand Marais, and 557 in tiny Grand Portage, the last stop before the Canadian side of the lake.

The iconic aerial lift bridge greets visitors to Duluth.

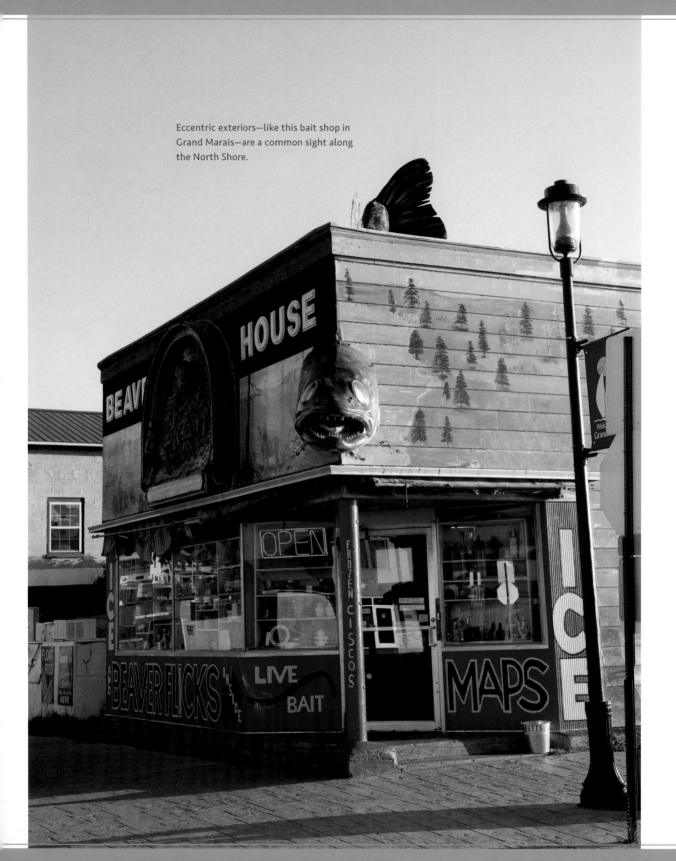

Eccentric exteriors—like this bait shop in Grand Marais—are a common sight along the North Shore.

Fine dining culture hangs on by its fingernails in places like Duluth and Grand Marais, serving up ambitious, locally sourced, world-beating haute cuisine in some places and tired, overpriced, cosmopolitan hotel fare in others. The closing of the high-end, high-concept Nokomis and Chez Jude restaurants—both well known and well regarded for their haute cuisine spins on local dining—signals the challenge of doing business on the North Shore. Locals, who are often thrifty, traditional, serious eaters with little time for fuss or ceremony, and tourists, who want coursed meals with modern treatments of high-end food, are hard to reconcile. Ignore one or the other at your own peril, but time seems to indicate that building on a local base of loyal regulars and then reaching out to the summer tourist crowd are more sustainable than the reverse approach. The best bet for those hoping to eat reliably great food is to follow the fresh fish and to find purveyors and restaurateurs who take approachable, affordably priced food to new heights, rather than those who lean on foams and glazes to dazzle the easily impressed.

This isn't to say that never the twain shall meet; at high-profile restaurants like the New Scenic Café and the now-closed Nokomis, I've had both mind-blowingly good local fare and head-scratchingly watered-down, overpriced mediocrities. Caveat emptor, although the search for passionately interpreted local food is often rewarded with vivid flavors and windows into what North Shore food culture could one day become.

ARRIVING IN DULUTH

The climate and landscape shift palpably on the drive to Duluth from the Twin Cities on Interstate 35. As we travel north, the air feels cleaner, the trees tend more and more toward evergreens, and the water has a more distinct sparkle to it. And we start to feel some of the most noticeable trappings of civilization fall away. The endless rings of strip malls and housing developments, chain restaurants ranging from fast-food to steakhouses, and reliable cell phone coverage all begin to recede as we clear the metropolitan area.

On our way up from the Twin Cities, we stop at Gordy's Hi-Hat in Cloquet and are pleasantly surprised. Gordy Lundquist himself is working the counter, helping to stem the roaring tide of tourists who rush to the front of the restaurant in search of lunch. That Lundquist is in his eighties and still slinging burgers is impressive. Equally impressive are the hand-pattied burgers themselves, which are (in the best possible sense of the word) culinary fossils, perfectly preserved pieces of classic American road food built right from good ingredients. Onions are peeled and sliced on-site to create the restaurant's buttermilk-and-pancake-battered onion rings, which are regionally famous.

We try a California burger, and the bun is thick but light, the patty thin but juicy, and the balance of tomatoes and lettuce pitched correctly, making each bite a mix of bright and smoky, acidic and bready. It's damn good. The accompanying blackberry shake is packed with fruit and is, consequently, impossible to suck through the straw—the thing clogs right up with bits of berries. For a shake, it's almost austere. There's little sugary flavor to it, and the natural flavor of the fruit dominates the ice cream. It's legitimately refreshing, and so legitimately refreshed, we make way onward toward Duluth.

Gordy's Hi-Hat in Cloquet serves one of the best hamburgers in the region.

The WPA Guide to Minnesota likens Duluth to "a Lilliputian village in a mammoth rock garden," a characterization that captures the massive, rocky nature of the surrounding countryside and the condensed feel of this industrial Lake Superior harbor. On the one hand, mining, shipping, and timber—all industries that bring jobs and can deplete and damage the environment—built the city. On the other hand, Duluth has a foothold in the knowledge economy with the presence of University of Minnesota Duluth while also being a gateway to nature. So the city presents a pleasant contradiction: a hub for learning, wilderness tourism, and lake adventures that also happens to be an industrial center for resource-draining, polluting businesses. The schizophrenic nature of the area can be felt just by walking around Canal Park, the city's amiably walkable tourist district, where shops selling framed photos of the lake or bags of saltwater taffy are overlooked by the towering aerial lift bridge, massive tankers, and the surrounding infrastructure required to move great quantities of material in an orderly fashion.

Gordy's Hi-Hat, 415 Sunnyside Drive, Cloquet, 218-879-6125.
www.gordys-hihat.com

A NEW BREED OF SMOKEHOUSE

NORTHERN WATERS SMOKEHAUS, DULUTH

Perhaps no single establishment exemplifies the "industry meets tourism" vibe of Canal Park more skillfully than Northern Waters Smokehaus, which has one foot squarely in the region's working-class past with its smoked fish and one foot squarely in the present with its sophisticated, urban, tourist-friendly menu.

The shop brings together commercial fishing and leisure dining and unites humble local food traditions with high-end modern technique and presentation. Testament to the shop's success is the line of customers that extends from its small shop out into the building's hallway and, sometimes, onto the deck of the DeWitt-Seitz Marketplace building. The combination of world-class ingredients sourced with care and clamorous crowds of locals and tourists alike makes this Duluth sandwich and meat shop feel far more like a Manhattan deli than the typical north-country diner.

Northern Waters Smokehaus owner Eric Goerdt proudly serves a plate of smoked fish at his shop in Duluth's Canal Park neighborhood.

Proprietor Eric Goerdt grew up in Iowa and fished Lake Michigan. His father "messed around" with smoking fish, a first blip of activity that would put the art of smoking onto Goerdt's radar. He moved with the U.S. Coast Guard to Duluth in 1995 and took his career in a different direction. "I bought a commercial smokehouse and started smoking fishes for different restaurants in the area," says Goerdt. "That was actually 1998, and I'd just go to the Chef's Association meetings with smoked fish and say, 'Would you guys like to put this on your menu?'"

Although his setting and most of his ingredients are North Shore, his style is imported. "I learned how to smoke in the style of the Pacific Northwest in Alaska," says Goerdt. "It's called 'kippering.' It's slightly different from the type of smoking they do up here. I thought there'd be a niche in the market for this type of smoked fish."

Kippering allows for more control than the traditional smokehouse approach of hanging fish over open flames. As Goerdt describes it, "It's like a cross between cold and hot smoking. You want that fish to dry. We'll pull it out of the brine, and we'll dry it overnight in a walk-in cooler until it gets very, very tacky. And then we put it in a real low-temperature smokehouse, 100 degrees. You gradually step up the temperature during the smoking process. We go from 100 to 125 to 140 to 150 to 160. And what that does is it allows for pellicle formation."

The pellicle is the shell-like golden skin that forms on the outside of the fish as smoke sticks to the dry tackiness of the fish's exterior. The result is one of the most beautiful and savory food products you'll likely ever taste. A thoughtful application of technique and heat takes a raw piece of natural protein and transforms it into a durable, delicate, high-cuisine realization of the flavor of the lake. "If you gradually raise the heat, you're not going to force the moisture and protein out of the fish," says Goerdt. "And then you'll end up with a fully cooked product, but it's really going to be moister on the inside. That slow step of temperature is called kippering."

FINE TUNING AND THE ART OF SMOKE

That sense of control—the ability to isolate variables and turn out a carefully crafted, high-end product—is a perfect parallel with many of Wisconsin's smaller craft creameries or some of the region's microbreweries. As those businesses do, Goerdt reinjects

MEZZE AT NORTHERN WATERS SMOKEHAUS

Northern Waters Smokehaus proprietor Eric Goerdt made a mixed plate of tastes for us before we hit the road: salamini, featuring great fennel flavor, a perfect (mild) level of salt, and a bit of sharpness and earthiness; lonzino, with the meaty flavor and real delicacy of texture, not sinewy; chorizo, with a spicy bump at the end of the flavor profile; and smoked king salmon, rich with the essential flavor of salmon, a bit of smoke, and a mildly sweet, lacquered exterior.

Visiting Goerdt's "microsmokery" was a great kickoff to the trip and a nice counterpoint to interviewing the guys at Fitger's, a lakeside brewery whose story is intertwined with that of Duluth.

old-fashioned craft into what could be a soulless, mass-marketed approach to food creation. His fusion of specialized knowledge and hours of labor leaves something fleeting but profound in its wake.

As Goerdt tells it, "In my mind's eye I had a vision of a little gourmet shop. I think about our operation as a micro-smokery, like a microbrewery. I love smoking fish, but I also love making liver pâté and I love making salami and I love making bacon, and so, and much like a microbrewery, I feel like we can dabble in all kinds of different arts. I didn't want to be a full-sized smoked fish house because that's boring. Because I like to do everything else."

Goerdt uses the word *dabble*, but it's not quite right—his meat is serious. His salamini won the coveted "golden pig" grand prize in an annual charcuterie contest put on by Armandino Batali, a world-renowned meat artisan who happens to be the father of celebrity chef Mario Batali. (Of Batali, Goerdt says, "There's only a handful of people making salami like this in the country, and he's considered one of the greats.")

The national food Web site CHOW.com praised the "mellow smoky flavor and natural sweetness" of his smoked lake trout and whitefish. The shop has been featured on Guy Fieri's "Diners, Drive-Ins and Dives" (and for the record, it is really none of those three things). And customers go nuts for his stuff, too—online reviews on sites like Yelp are jammed with five-star raves.

AN INSPIRING BEGINNING

An Alaskan hunter taught Goerdt many of the basics for curing and preserving meat. Starting with bison pastrami in 2002, Goerdt was hooked, and he developed a menu that would come to revolve around house-smoked turkey breasts, bacon, and bison pastrami. A visit to Vancouver illuminated for Goerdt the glorious potential of sophisticated cured meats. "At Granville Island Public Market there was a salami maker . . . and his shop and it was like a Renaissance painting. It was like, beautiful, moldy saucissons, duck prosciuttos, boar prosciutto, everything hanging in baskets, and it was just absolutely stunning. And I knew salami was part of the art of sausage making, and I was like, 'I've got to learn how to do that.'"

Iowa State University is nationally known for its meat science program, so Goerdt took a dry sausage production class there to learn the science behind the art. "When I went to school," says Goerdt, "I went with a guy that's making the salami for Mario Batali's restaurants and Mario and his dad, Armandino, said, 'You've got to go to this school or you can't do it.'"

"And then I just read everything there was to read about salami production, you know . . . all the books and stuff that are out there," he adds. "And then just slowly but surely started to define a process."

Award-winning salamini on display at Northern Waters Smokehaus.

When you talk to food artisans anywhere in the world, the shores of Lake Superior included, they talk about their work as a fusion of art and science, a crossroads between the intuitive and the quantifiable. The more trained you are, and the more you understand the chemistry and biology of what you're doing, the more of the "intuitive" stuff is revealed to have sound scientific underpinnings. But there's always an interplay.

"You really have to pay attention to the science," says Goerdt. "Salami production, just to make a long story short, it was a way to preserve meats prior to refrigeration." The Ojibwa of Lake Superior have an ancient history of preserving meats and fruits through smoking, both for later consumption and to enhance the flavor. Certainly the French voyageurs, whose early explorations around the lake helped open up the north country for timber and mineral exploitation, knew the value of sausages. Anyone who has traveled long distances under their own power understands the value of smoked fish and cured meat—it's compact, it's filling, it's nutritious, and after a day of exertion, it's astonishingly tasty.

"The challenge is you're not going to cook this pork, but you're going to make it edible or safe to eat and shelf stable," says Goerdt. "They used to do it with wild bacteria; it's very much like brewing beer. We actually ferment, we ferment the meat like you do in beer production."

In the early days of meat curing, bacteria from previous batches would be used, much as modern bakers pass sourdough starter from bread loaf to bread loaf, keeping the "mother culture" alive in the interim. The method, called "backslapping," is now less prevalent but is still used in some artisan settings. Rather than use backslapping, Goerdt works with carefully harvested and preserved culture specifically created for his cured meat.

Goerdt imports bacterial culture taken from salamis in southern Europe. It arrives frozen, at which point Goerdt equilibrates it in water and puts it in his mix, adding spices, curing salts, and salt. The pH of the mixture dips below 5, a level inhospitable to botulinums, trichinae, and other harmful microflora. His sausages ferment at a temperature of seventy-five degrees. The result, in Goerdt's case, is sausages that recall the earthier varieties predominant in southern Europe, as opposed to the tarter, snappier sorts favored in Germany and parts north—think summer sausage with its massive acidic bite.

"You can check out our lonzino—it's our prosciutto that we make out of pork loin. And it's fantastic. Like a brewery, every product that you kick out has to be consistently good, so you can't just willy-nilly throw [stuff] out there, so we've got the chorizo and we've got the salamini down."

Having the making of aged sausages down on an artisan level means that you don't take the kind of chemical shortcuts used by big companies making massive batches of sausage on a fast timetable.

THE DEPTH, SOUL, AND EARTH CHARM OF AGED MEAT

"There's nothing that replicates time and good bacteria," says Goerdt. "The flavor profile [of commercial mass-batch aged sausage] is so flat compared to this earthy, beautiful thing." That earthy beauty makes a good base for some of Northern Waters' sandwiches, including the Italiensk, which includes salami (a mix of the shop's salamini and pepperoni) with ham, pickles, olives, onions, tomatoes, provolone, plus oil and vinegar on a hero roll, garnished with black pepper.

My personal favorite, though, is the Cajun Finn, so called because it brings together Cajun seasoning with Finnish-inspired smoked fish. "It's our Cajun-style smoked salmon, on a bun with scallion, blue cheese, roasted red peppers, and pepperoncinis," says Goerdt. The combination of cool, funky cheese, smoky peppers and fish, acidic and spicy pepperoncinis, and hot Cajun spicing is a flavor bomb and easily one of the ten best bites on the North Shore. Another of shop's claims to fame is Sitka sushi, an Asian-style gravlax made from wild sockeye salmon that's cleaned and cured with salt, sugar, lemon juice, and fresh ginger. Sliced razor thin, it's teamed up with cabbage and pickled ginger.

The shop smokes Atlantic salmon, and lake trout and whitefish from Lake Superior, and all of them make for good eating. Goerdt is particularly proud of the lake trout, which come in as whole fish. Goerdt splits the fish in half, leaving the bones in to retain moisture, and then chunks the fish up. The pieces are then brined and rubbed with dark brown sugar, then left overnight—the process transforms the fish into a rich, succulent treat that practically melts in your mouth.

Goerdt says that he isn't worried that he'll run out of local fish in his lifetime. He has a positive outlook about the current health of the lake's fisheries, driven by the

Making sausage is a labor-intensive process at Northern Waters Smokehaus.

expansion of the herring population, which he identifies as the key, base baitfish in the lake upon which the other populations feed for survival.

Duluth–Superior is also, in its own way, the base of the lake. While Thunder Bay proper has the largest population of any city on the lake, the Duluth–Superior metropolitan area is the largest by a factor of two, and the dominant port. From Goerdt's perspective, a retail shopkeeper and food artisan serving high-end sandwiches to locals and tourists, the area is doing well.

"Business is fantastic," he says. "It's a beautiful place. And the people that come here, they love Lake Superior. And I've found that capitalizing on what is great in our region, that's what people want. Like when you travel somewhere else. You go to Hawaii you're going to eat mahimahi. You go to Duluth, you're going to have whitefish. There's a lot of people that really realize what a resource this lake is. It's like an ocean. It's beautiful. It's the cleanest of the Great Lakes."

Goerdt sees himself as part of a movement in Duluth specifically and on the North Shore more generally: food artisans embracing local flavor and using fine technique to bring it up to a world-class experience.

"Right after we moved here, the [Fitger's] brewhouse started up," he says. "It just seems like there's a lot of really unique businesses and eateries here that are kind of capitalizing on our region and making for a healthy economy."

Goerdt's shop has become woven into the fabric of life in Duluth. "I see the same people every day," he says. "It's really . . . like *Cheers*. If people want to get in, they start making the sandwich exactly what they want. They'll start making it with extra cilantro, and we know that Roger likes that sandwich."

The locals, Goerdt explains, bring in the tourists. By capturing the local trade, he ensured himself good word of mouth and the boost that out-of-city money can bring.

"I notice that people who come up here from Minneapolis come up two or three times a year. And they're like, 'Oh, let's just go up there for the weekend. Cool down. Let's go to the lake.' It's almost like a playground for people from Minneapolis. We have regulars from Minneapolis. So that's kind of neat."

"You start with good products, and you put love and time into them," says Goerdt. "You have fun doing it, and I kind of feel like we're an asset to the community. I never feel like I'm going to work."

Northern Waters Smokehaus, 394 South Lake Avenue, Suite 106, Duluth, 218-724-7307. www.northernwaterssmokehaus.com

BREWING ON THE NORTH SHORE

FITGER'S BREWHOUSE, DULUTH

The recent craft-brewing boom that has swept the United States from coast to coast has also made its mark on the North Shore, but Duluth is no stranger to brewing. Long before its current incarnation as the leader of the North Shore craft beer movement, Fitger's got its start in 1859 when four unemployed locals acquired a site on First Street and Washington Avenue near a little stream they named Brewery Creek. The Duluth Brewing and Malting Company formed in 1896 and by 1933 was one of only ten breweries in the United States both producing malt for its own use and selling the excess. It became best known for Karlsbrau, a popular label that survived the brewery's demise and was sold to Cold Spring, where it was brewed into the 1980s. Also, the Peoples Brewing Company had a good fifty-year run, from 1906 to 1957, producing Peoples (later Stag) beer and Olde English 600 malt liquor, which would even-

Fitger's brewmaster Dave Hoops (left) and owner Tim Nelson (right).

tually transcend its Duluth origins, jumping through multiple ownership changes and losing its 600 in favor of 800, and become a hip-hop icon.

Since those early days, the concept of beer has changed. No longer a mere working-man's beverage, craft brew is sought after and valued for complex layers of flavor akin to that of wine. Interest in local craft brew has trickled into even the fine dining scene on the North Shore. Special restaurant dinners pairing fine food with wine are old hat; dinners that take the same approach using craft brew are a newer phenomenon but have started to percolate through the American haute cuisine community in recent years, presenting an exciting new set of challenges and rewards for restaurateurs.

As a starting point for experiencing local beer married to local food, we attended a pairing dinner that matched the food of (the now-closed) Chez Jude in Grand Marais with the beers of St. Paul–based Summit Brewing. Judi Barsness, owner and executive chef of Chez Jude, spoke about the meal in geographic terms that would make any Upper Midwesterner proud:

> This is truly a Minnesota harvest celebration. All of the ingredients on this menu have been locally sourced from Minnesota and northern Wisconsin, some of them right here from Grand Marais—the wild rice is from a local harvester, and some of the herbs are from our kitchen garden, and some are from local growers who supply us. It was just a perfect match for us to match these ingredients with Minnesota's greatest beers, from Summit Brewing.

The menu we dined from read like this, and it's a nice summary of how local food and beer can pair up in a way worthy of a special occasion:

Bison Wild Rice Bratwurst with Beer & Brown Mustard Aioli paired with Summit India Pale Ale

Mussels Steamed in Beer paired with Summit Pilsener

Wood Fire Roasted Pekin Duck Breast with a Honey Thyme Scented Red Ale Glace (paired, of course, with Summit Red Ale)

An intermezzo of Summit Pale Ale Cranberry Sorbet

Beer Braised Short Ribs of Beef with Horseradish Creme Fraiche paired with Summit Octoberfest

Dessert of Chocolate Stout Torte, Chocolate Stout Toffee Chip Ice Cream and a pairing of Summit Great Northern Porter

Summit's founder and head brewer Mark Stutrud put the brewing industry into historical terms that gave context to the current boom in great local craft beers. In the mid-1980s, when he got started, there was little on the landscape beyond macrobrews and a few imports like Bass, Anchor, and Guinness. Now, hundreds of breweries in the Upper Midwest compete to define the flavor not just of their region or state but their city and county, echoing the richness of Europe's many small artisan producers.

Summit made a major impact on Minnesota brewing by blazing new trails in flavor, setting a precedent that breweries on the North Shore—Lake Superior, the reincarnated Fitger's, the newly established Castle Danger Brewery—have been able to follow.

Stutrud put it like this: "Back in 1986 when people were asking us about why we made Extra Pale Ale taste the way it did, they'd ask: 'Why didn't you make Bass Ale, something like that?' And we'd say, 'Because it already exists. Why do something that's already there?'"

THE REBIRTH OF AMERICAN BEER

Beer in America has gone from careful craft to mass-marketed commodity and back again in the span of 150 years. Fitger's brewery in Duluth represents the whole arc of the story. Over the course of the late nineteenth and early twentieth centuries, Fitger's became the biggest brewery in Duluth before running into the wall that was Prohibition.

"Prohibition stopped everything," says Fitger's brewmaster, Dave Hoops. We're sampling a selection of the brewpub's current beers amid the din of a full house. Known for its rotating, house-made craft brew selections and an array of simple but passionately executed bar food (including a surprisingly luscious Harvest Moon wild-rice veggie burger that is a regional favorite), Fitger's is the anchor of the hotel and retail complex that shares its name. Lake Superior sits right outside the window, making it one of the most scenic places to drink, nosh, or stay for visitors to Duluth.

The vibe is cozy, and the in-house tap handles are mesmerizing—they're hand-blown glass art objects created by local glassmaker Jes Durfee. "He's as good at making glass as we are at making beer," says Fitger's co-owner Tim Nelson.

Handblown glass taps mark the offerings at the historic Fitger's Brewhouse in Duluth.

Before Prohibition, Fitger's was making German-style light lagers, an easy-drinking beer style that's a forerunner of modern "macrobrew" like Budweiser and Miller, minus the rice or corn "adjuncts" that many craft beer drinkers look upon as a betrayal of the beverage's simple German roots. "They were probably the equivalent of the Helles style of beer," says Hoops. "The adjunct-laden, dumbed-down beer wasn't produced by this brewery, at least until later."

Fitger's stayed open during Prohibition and hung on—barely—by making soda and molasses candy. Eventually, after repeal, the brewery started making beer again, rising to a position of regional prominence in the late 1950s and 1960s. "They were

THE BEER OF BOREALIS FERMENTERY

www.borealisfermentery.com

"Big beer, big lake, small brewery" is the slogan of Borealis Fermentery, a one-man crusade to bring real Belgian-style beers to the North Shore. Brewer Ken Thiemann nearly died after falling from the roof of the Belgian monastery–inspired, straw-bale home and brewery that he built himself, but since recovering, he has been producing (small amounts of) the most subtle, balanced, and intriguing Belgian beer around. You can't visit the brewery, but you can taste his work at restaurants like the New Scenic Café and Tycoon's Alehouse in Duluth.

producing about a hundred thousand barrels a year, which is huge," Hoops says. Huge, of course, is relative in a world of mega breweries and consolidation. "Now that was about the time when Budweiser got serious about what they were doing, and they started buying and squeezing out all the regional breweries. Fitger's went from being a huge force to slowly tapering down, sold, and stopped producing beer for good in 1972."

But as the face of the North Shore changed, development opportunities opened up that well suited the historic Fitger's building by the lake. "In the late eighties a group from Duluth bought it," Hoops recalls. "The city built them this parking garage, and they renovated the hotel and put some money into it, and quickly it grew into what it is now. It's a successful mall, it's got four restaurants in it, and the hotel. We opened in 1995."

The space that formerly held a Rocky Rococo's pizza parlor was transformed. "The two owners had an idea when they were out in Colorado traveling. They saw a few brewpubs that were flourishing even then," Hoops recalls. "They had the idea of opening a beer bar with a really cool vibe and a Colorado ski-town feel, and they did that."

Hoops is from a family well known regionally for its brewing expertise. His brother, Mike, is head brewer at the award-winning Town Hall Brewery in Minneapolis. When Dave was making wine in San Francisco in the late 1980s, Mike visited him, and the history of Upper Midwestern beer changed. "My brother came out to visit me and brewed his first batch in his life on my stove there, and then we continued in two different ways," says Dave Hoops. "My brother became a very accomplished home brewer and starting working here as a bartender when it opened, and he said to the owners, 'You might want to consider opening a brewery . . .' Neither of [the owners] had any background, but Mike pitched it to them and they listened, they bought a used system and installed it all themselves, and started going through the process . . .

"Mike had built the brewery and went from a multitap bar to a fledgling brewery in 1997. Tim jumped in with Mike, and the two of them began brewing beer there."

The beers that Fitger's were founded on are largely still around: Big Boat Stout, Witchtree ESB, and Lighthouse Golden still grace the taps. "There were four or five beers that are still around today," says Hoops. "We've maybe improved them a little bit, but they're more or less similar. There were only five or six lines of beer then." Now, Fitger's typically serves twenty to twenty-five different kinds of beers—all made in house—at any given time.

The transition from Mike Hoops to Dave Hoops was a smooth one. "I showed up in '99. At the end of '99 I was brewing with the Pyramid brewery at that point," says Hoops. "Mike left to go to the Upper Peninsula, and he said, 'Hey Timmy! You want a good brewer?' and Tim called me, and we started chatting, and next thing I know, we're moving to Minnesota." Hoops was pleased to make the jump back to the Upper Midwest. "One of the things that we wanted was to raise our kids here for a better quality of life [than California], but there were no jobs," recalls Hoops. "So here I had a chance to come to a fledgling brewery that was on the upswing."

SPARING NO EXPENSE, TAKING THEIR TIME

The philosophy of Fitger's is simple but intrinsically challenging. "I brew what I like to drink," says Hoops. "We started, right off the bat, using the best ingredients in the world, creating beers of great character sparing zero expense. We kind of defined the Duluth/north Minnesota scene—we brew beers that would fit in really well in San Francisco but also fit in really well up here."

Tanks of beer await dispensing at Fitger's Brewhouse.

"One thing I see you guys doing is a real nod to traditionalism—I see you doing stuff that's traditional in German styles," says Nelson.

"We don't filter anything, we don't believe in it," says Hoops. "We make a lot of lager beers, which few brewpubs do because of the time and expense involved. And we also are blessed with the greatest beer-drinking culture in the state, hands down. The people here embrace us—we've kind of become an institution. We are Duluth, and Duluth is us. We do everything the old way, and everything we do takes more time."

If you write about food, you get used to people—everybody, regardless of what they do—claiming to use the best ingredients, sparing no expense. It's an appealing story, but it's worth pushing for details. I did, and Hoops supplied them.

"We only use two-row malt, which is much more expensive to produce," says Hoops. "We don't use adjuncts—we don't augment our sugars with rice or corn. We age our beers much longer than almost any other brewpub because we don't filter. We need time for our beers to clarify and for the flavors to develop, and that's a very expensive move right there. Where another brewery could put out a beer in three weeks, it has taken us six."

Time, of course, is money. Vintage wine, hard Italian cheese, and single malt scotch are all luxury items in part because of the months and years that go into making them. Fitger's doesn't sweat the expense and happily turns out a lager that takes twelve weeks to properly age out; the brewery uses between twelve and sixteen yeast strains each year, offering many varieties of beer, as compared to two or three that might be used by a smaller-scale conventional brewpub.

The brewing process at Fitger's is unusual for more than simply quality-control reasons. It's spread out throughout the Fitger's complex, with tanks squatting and towering in odd corners and rooms throughout the building. "We have forty-four different tanks in this little tiny building because we have so many beers," says Hoops. Running from tank to tank keeps the staff (three full-time and three part-time workers) plenty busy.

The connection between the new, West Coast–inspired Fitger's and the city of Duluth goes far beyond the name and the historic building. "[Tim's] whole philosophy from the day we started has been local first. It's here because [the owners] love Duluth, they love the water—they're creative people," says Hoops. From the day Fitger's opened, free live entertainment has been part of the mix, a crucial fragment of the equation that makes the establishment a pillar of Duluth nightlife and culture. Locally grown hops complement the Duluth water that goes into the beer, and local fruit graces the brewpub's fruit beer. "We have the apple beer with apples from Bayfield," says Hoops. "Blueberry beer with berries from Bayfield. Cherries from Door County. Raspberries from here in town."

The holistic cultural vision for the brewery is just part of a larger, boundary-pushing aesthetic that makes Fitger's the force that it is in Duluth and on the North Shore of Superior. From its German-made filling machine that fills growlers under pressure, to its barrel-aged beers program, to its tap handles and historic setting, to its music program, to its dedication to craft ingredients, the brewery is a pacesetter.

It also runs tied houses, establishments "tied" to the Fitger's brewery through the beers they offer, at Duluth's Burrito Union, the Redstar Lounge, and the newly opened Tycoons restaurant and bar. ("Duluth had more millionaires per capita than anywhere else back in the day," notes Nelson.) "We want to continue on with this movement of craft beer," says Nelson. "Dave and I have plans to keep brewing more and bigger and better—we believe in what we're doing."

Fitger's Brewhouse, 600 East Superior Street, Duluth, 218-279-2739. www.brewhouse.net

A NORTH SHORE MICROROASTER

DULUTH COFFEE COMPANY, DULUTH

Lake Superior has an intimate relationship with coffee. When the region is blanketed by winter, as it is many months of the year, the desire for something hot and caffeinated moves from a luxury to a necessity. At one point Duluth was home to one of the largest coffee roasters in the country. The Rust-Parker Company had an annual roasting capacity of 2.5 million pounds and distributed nationally under the Table King and Omar brands. The company was liquidated in 1947, but at least one major company remains in the Twin Ports area: the Andresen-Ryan Company (famous for its Arco brand of coffee) still roasts and ships its product to a loyal following in Minnesota, Wisconsin, and Michigan.

The Duluth Spice and Coffee Company was established in 1893, and while it has

been long defunct, its name lives on, in a way. Coffee roaster Eric Faust founded the Duluth Coffee Company in 2009 with the idea of "microroasting"—akin to microbrewing—small batches, with careful hand selection of ingredients and careful babying of the process to ensure precise results. Faust uses a custom-built roaster from the US Roaster Corp in Oklahoma that combines enameled-metal beauty evocative of an Italian sports car with glowing green and red lights you would associate with a factory workstation.

"They build their roasters like the old German-style ones," says Faust, as he prepares to fire up the machine. "All the roasters you see in [the Minneapolis-based

Duluth Coffee Company owner and roaster Eric Faust carefully prepares a batch of beans.

chain] Dunn Bros and stuff use infrared heat; this one uses atmospheric burners. It gives you more control."

He pops open the machine to display a concentrated bank of blue flame jets that spread out into yellow-white gouts that lap against the bottom of the drum. "For an inexperienced roaster, it's very intense," he says. "If you don't know how to use the machine, it's a lot more difficult." Faust compares it to cooking over an open fire, as opposed to cooking in a microwave. "I work with just the heat and air control," he says. "It's a very traditional way to roast. There's no computer, I don't set a profile. . . . You go to a place like Peace Coffee (a major local roaster in Minneapolis), and they have the big computer screen, and they'll set their temperature on that."

Batches are small. Faust roasts just six or seven pounds at a time, factoring in the atmosphere, humidity, and temperature in his chic-but-welcoming café and roast-ery in downtown Duluth. "I roasted coffee this morning, and it went in on a colder roaster, and I was able to feel that based on sight and sound," he says. "And so I'll hit different benchmarks in the roast process, and I'll react to them, whereas a larger roaster will have so much volume they won't be able to feel that as much."

THE COMMON LANGUAGE OF THE FOOD ARTISAN

Everything Faust says would be familiar to a craft brewer, a meat artisan, or a master cheesemaker. Small batches of product can be steered by hand to account for varia-tions in weather, product quality, client taste, and other factors, and the result can be the creation of great food rather than something merely edible. Faust says that a twenty-five-pound roast batch is as large as he wants to tackle at one time. Larger than that, it becomes difficult to "feel" where the coffee is and control the quality of the roast. His current setup roasts twenty pounds an hour, and he sells about sixty to ninety pounds a week.

When Faust's coffee arrives from abroad, he takes the unroasted beans out of their burlap and puts them into a large plastic container to preserve their moisture. The burlap lets the beans breathe and prevents rot during shipping, while allowing customs easy access to the contents of the bag. But once the beans are ready to be roasted, Faust wants their moisture content to stabilize, thus the less breathable plas-tic bins.

As a young entrepreneur peddling a specialty product, Faust is a small fish in the medium-sized pond that is the local coffee market, but he has been aggressively pitching local restaurants and coffeehouses to carry his beans, backed by his easily accessible expertise.

As Faust roasts his beans, the small outbuilding slowly but surely fills up with a powerful aroma evocative of a campfire in the wilderness. Combined with the sound of the beans in the drum and the roar of the flames, the overall experience is mesmerizing. "This is full blast, so the heat is just barreling into it," says Faust. "I'll push it into the first crack, when the moisture breaks and the process turns from drying to caramelization. The second crack is the wooden structure burning like a campfire—it's good in certain coffees but not others."

As the coffee roasts, Faust talks about the sense of place that defines his business. "It's an old blue-collar town, and that's still what a lot of the jobs are," he says. "You go to west Duluth and everything is still named for the town: Duluth Mirror and Glass, Duluth Tire . . . I just thought there should be a Duluth Coffee Company."

While micro drum roasting of coffee is common in the Twin Cities, Faust stands alone in his part of the state. He says that he sees himself as an educator and that part of that education is teaching his customers that every bean is different and every roast—even the currently unfashionable darker roasts—has its place.

Faust, who has written about coffee for national publications and worked at the well-respected Black Sheep Coffee Cafe in South Saint Paul, is soft spoken. But he is also proud of his approach and style, which involves shifting to darker roasts when it makes a more pleasing end product for the consumer. "[Artisanal] coffee roasters down there [in the Twin Cities] are roasting coffee too light," he says, engaging with one of the trends running wild with the sometimes hyperfussy, scientific equipment–mad coffee shops often referred to as "third wave" by watchers of coffee industry trends. "The last time I was at [a third-wave café and roastery in Minneapolis] the barista was talking about their coffee and how it had 'this great tomato soup note,' and I was thinking, 'Really? Why would I want tomato soup in my coffee, that seems like a problem.'"

That's another way in which Duluth Coffee Company's product echoes the style of many of the newer midwestern microbreweries. Rather than kicking out challenging, "extreme" beers (for example, the aggressive brews put out by Twin Cities–based

Surly Brewing), many of the newer brewers blend approachable, balanced flavor profiles with good ingredient sourcing and careful brewing techniques to create brews respected by the beer geeks but drinkable by the general public.

Faust packages his coffee in brown paper with an ink stamp on it. It's beyond simple, but it manages to look both economical and chic. "There's been this craze to use expensive packaging for coffee," he says, holding a bag of his beans in one hand. "I try to pay less than twenty cents a unit for the packaging. I had a quote done for a package with a logo and foil lining and the vacuum seal, and it was over a dollar a package. Instead, I purchased a stamp.

"I'm so small and my overhead's so low, and I'm selling coffee that's more expensive and doing OK. My margin is probably 20 percent lower than it should be. The business, I'm able to break even."

CINNAMON CAKE DOUGHNUT AT WORLD'S BEST DONUTS

10 Wisconsin Street, Grand Marais.
www.worldsbestdonutsmn.com

Are the World's Best Donuts the world's best doughnuts? Debatable, especially if you have tried my grandmother's homemade doughnuts. That said, this is a wonderful little doughnut shop located lakeside in Grand Marais, and the two items we tried (a glazed and a cinnamon cake doughnut) were both excellent. The cinnamon, in particular, is worth talking about: it was tender and relatively light, not overly sweet, and packed a real spice kick.

The glazed doughnut was similarly light on its feet and balanced, for a doughnut—sweet, yes, but not just a mass of melted sugar on a low-grade pastry. When doughnuts are made fresh on-site, the impact on flavor is massive, and the World's Best Donuts lend themselves brilliantly to a midmorning stroll along the shore of Lake Superior, coffee in hand.

For now, as a newcomer to the marketplace and the Lake Superior artisanal food community, Faust is doing his best to break in through his local specialty accounts and by evangelizing face-to-face whenever possible. "I sell at the farmers market over in Superior, and that's been really good," he says. "People are really curious about it. They like fresh roasted coffee."

Duluth Coffee Company, 105 East Superior Street, Duluth, 218-464-5025. www.duluthcoffeecompany.com

OLD SMOKE AND GOLDEN FISH

RUSS KENDALL'S SMOKEHOUSE, KNIFE RIVER

The connection between smoked fish and community is equally as obvious—or possibly more obvious—at Russ Kendall's Smokehouse in Knife River, Minnesota. The humble repository of some of the North Shore's richest local food history sits just twenty miles up the coast from Duluth on Highway 61. Once you drive the Avenue of the Saints (61 runs through St. Paul, St. Louis, and New Orleans) north from Duluth, your circle tour has officially kicked off. This Mississippi-hugging highway, immortalized by Bob Dylan, is a way to segue from the relative bustle of the Twin Ports of Duluth and Superior to the quiet of the lakeshore. Standing roadside near the little port of Knife River is Russ Kendall's Smokehouse, a sentry posted at the gateway to the wilder side of the lake.

We showed up at Russ Kendall's for our interview midmorning on a Wednesday, expecting that—like many retail shops in even densely populated urban areas—the place would be mostly empty and we could have a long, uninterrupted conversation with coproprietor Gordy Olson. Despite what seemed to be an empty highway, we had no such luck. The front door's bell rang like a Christmas carol, and Olson was called away two, three, possibly four different times to help address the crush of customers turning up for their fish. Some were tourists, but most weren't. This is how locals eat up here on the shore of the lake.

"What we do is part of the culture of this area," says Olson, who married into the North Shore fish business thirty-four years ago. "To the rest of the world, what we

Gordy Olson, coproprietor of Russ Kendall's Smokehouse in Knife River, displays a freshly smoked fish.

do is gourmet, but here it's meat and potatoes. That space [and here he points over to the humble dining area of the shop], we don't have any servers. People will just eat the smoked fish cold, on crackers, as finger food. We provide the space for people to do that."

Dressed down, Olson's smoked fish make for a weekday lunch or a tourist's picnic. Dressed up, they can be the anchor of a major celebration. "We do a lot of custom smoking," he says. "It shows up at weddings, and gives an ambiance—the large, smoked king salmon fillet, brilliant red. We do a lot of that.

"We live in Duluth, and it's not because of the great economic situation by any

means. You live up here because of the environment. We're part of that culture." Sustaining that culture, to Olson, means using local product whenever possible, and wild-caught exclusively. The result is a shop with products that reflect the landscape around it, a place where you can taste and appreciate the traditions of the North Shore.

"I don't do any imported fish," Olson says. "I do 100 percent wild-caught USA fish. In the future, if I have to do pond-raised Chilean fish, well, you got to do what you have to survive in this world." He adds, "There's no commercial harvest of any salmons on the Great Lakes for resale, so our salmons are Alaskan."

When Olson sources local fish, he starts as local as possible—with fishermen

The fish smoked on-site at Russ Kendall's is always freshly caught.

like Steve Dahl—and then works his way outward, into Wisconsin, or Michigan, or Canada, eventually going all the way around the lake depending on available supplies and the time of year. "One advantage that you have when you're dealing with very local fish is that when it comes out of the water, it's still wiggling—the quality's there," says Olson. "But the main thing for us is that you're putting food on your neighbor's table, and that's important."

Olson is heir to a long lakeside tradition. Russ Kendall's is nearly a hundred years old, dating back to William Kendall, "the original patriarch of the business," according to Olson, who established its patterns. As the story goes, one day in 1918 Kendall was bringing fish down the shore to Duluth for sale when his REO Speedwagon truck broke down. He set up a fish stand along the roadside and managed to sell the whole load in half a day, thereby sowing the seed for the business.

Generations of smokehouses came and went, first built as primitive log outbuildings, then made from finished wood, then finally fire-resistant brick. The method of smoking, however, has changed little in the many years that the shop has sat by the roadside in Knife River. "We still smoke over open fires as they did," says Olson. "The original people here, the Anishinaabe, were the ones who taught us, our family, William Kendall how to smoke fish. Having said that, the process we use is a Scottish hot-smoking process, and whether they both evolved at the same time or the Anishinaabe adopted this from whatever, that I don't know."

You might think that the advent of modern food safety standards would have changed the way Kendall's does business, but no, the old process was up to modern standards. "A few years ago we came under federal health regulations (HACCP)," says Olson, "and we were documenting salt content and things like that, and it was kind of amazing to me that a centuries-old process had enough ability to know where the health parameters were. The hot, smoking process kills bacteria.

"The only difference is the simple documentation, which was just a piece of paper."

Tradition and community notwithstanding, becoming a fish merchant wasn't Olson's original intention. But when he married his wife, Kristi Kendall, he married the smokehouse as well, and he let his successful marine mechanic profession fall by the wayside.

A TYPICAL "SMOKE DAY"

The stress of the fish-smoking business starts after the fish have been caught and dressed by the fisherman. After the gills and guts have been removed, the fish can be graded, brined, and stored in a refrigeration unit. "And then it comes from the refrigeration unit into the smoke ovens, and that's a smoke day for us," says Olson. "So we got a brine day, we got a smoke day. When it goes into the smoke ovens there, it takes a day for it go through that process—typically ten hours. Then it goes into the cooler, and it's packaged to be sold."

The business is a steady one for Russ Kendall's but not lucrative, and there was a time when Olson worried that his shop might not make it. "It was kind of scary a few years back, when we were kind of the last man standing," he recalls. "We were doing good. But then everybody else disappears for one reason or another, and pretty soon we're sitting here all by ourselves, worrying . . . when are we next? But now we're seeing it start to come back."

The recovery of lake fish from the collapse of their population numbers in the mid-twentieth century is part of the reason for Olson's optimism. He sees a lake fish population at an all-time high, relative to his thirty-four years of experience in the business. Mine tailings, smelt, and lamprey have all done damage to the fragile fish stocks of the lake, but those problems have largely passed into history. As a result, he thinks that it's time to allow more people to fish the North Shore. The twenty-five licensed commercial fishermen on the North Shore, he argues, could sustain more competition, and the business could use the refreshing addition of new blood.

"We're taking a raw product, and we're generating cash from it," says Olson. "Between Duluth and the Canadian border the economic impact of our industry is between fourteen and fifteen million dollars, and for a very rural area it's very important."

He moves on to talk about the art of smoking. At Russ Kendall's, it's done with local maple wood. And while many will swear that Kendall's does the best smoking on the North Shore (or the whole lake, for that matter), for Olson, the proof is in the fish. "The bottom line is you do the best you can, and the person who'll be the judge is the customer," he says. "Being the self-proclaimed best at anything is meaningless."

As for the act of smoking itself, he holds up ten fingers to demonstrate his point.

Fish dangle delicately from the rafters inside the smokers at Russ Kendall's.

"This is the smoking process . . . and this much is science [here he holds up six fingers], and this much is art [and here he holds up four fingers]."

While my photographer followed Olson for a tour of the smokehouse and an opportunity to catch the process as it unfolded, I chatted with Russ Kendall's Smokehouse worker Rory Kuehn. He has been smoking fish here for more than three decades, and he described the challenges of using a traditional smoking process. "There's hot spots and cold spots," he says, "and you have to watch the cisco, they're little and they're last fish in, first fish out. If you don't watch them, they can burn right up. And when I say burned up, the public wouldn't even notice—I'm not talking black.

"I'm talking about you'd lose too much of the weight. Ciscos are really tight on the profit margins, they're small little fish. They're really fatty. You can easily lose too much weight if you cook out the fat. There's really no room for error." Ciscos are Kuehn's favorite smoked fish ("There's more fat in it, there's more flavor"), but "the best eating fish out of the lake, I'd say, is herring."

The actual act of smoking fish is fundamentally beautiful. To smoke fish is to take fire, a wild, chaotic chemical reaction that symbolizes both warmth and destruction, and breathe it into delicate flesh, coloring and coating the fish and rendering it durable, deeply but thoughtfully flavored, and more valuable. To look upon rows of bronzing fish absorbing the light, fragrant smoke is to look upon art. The art is a delicate dance—go too far with the smoke and flames, and you're left with something tough and dry. Do it right, and the fish is tender and delicate but stable, and smoky without being ashy or overly strong. Like all of the great culinary arts—brewing, baking, winemaking, cooking, and cheesemaking—smoking fish can be described as science defined by temperatures and lengths of time, but there is always an art to it. It's a gut sense that guides the process, protects the fish from the fire, and ensures the kind of product that people will come back for, year after year.

Despite the depiction by Eric Goerdt of Northern Waters Smokehaus of traditional smoking as less precise and more prone to creating a dried-out product—no doubt true, as a rule—the fish at Russ Kendall's that we sampled was moist, delectable, and rich in flavor. Decades of working with smoke and fire have led to an understanding between the Kendall-Olsons and the process, and that understanding has resulted in profoundly savory food with one of the quintessential flavors of the lake.

Olson's daughters work at the shop during the busy summer season, and his son,

Cody, has taken a full-time interest in the business, ensuring a smooth succession to the next generation. "He seems to have taken an interest in the business, otherwise he wouldn't be here," says Olson. "Straight up. There's a lot easier things to do."

Easier, certainly. More meaningful? Perhaps not. "We do have a lot of fun with this business, we have fun talking to people. Each and every person who walks through that door is here to have a good time," says Olson, as customers stream in and out. "But when I was a boat mechanic, each and every person hated you . . . because their boat had broke down and you were costing them money. This business gives us a chance to see and do things most people never will."

Russ Kendall's Smokehouse, 149 Highway 61, Knife River, 218-834-5995. www.facebook.com/RussKendalls

CLEAN WATER, OLD BOATS, AND EVER-CHANGING SKIES

COMMERCIAL FISHING WITH STEVE DAHL, KNIFE RIVER

For fisherman Steve Dahl, reporting to work is a matter of motoring his weather-worn herring skiff out of the shelter of the Knife River Marina and making his way to his gill nets, which float near Knife Island in Lake Superior. On a clear, sunny July morning, as the sun's rays are breaking over the horizon and illuminating the rocks and gently lapping waves, the scene is as graceful as can be imagined, enough to set an atheist wondering or to nudge an agnostic toward belief.

Presume, for example, that you are not a morning person and that doing a ride-along with Dahl means a 5:15 A.M. hotel departure in Duluth in order to be out on the lake an hour later. And presume further that you're not at all fond of being out on the open water.

Even under these conditions—tired, grumpy, disoriented, green with fear, casting your eyes around for life preservers and finding only beaten-up old seat cushions as flat as an envelope—you are in awe of your majestic setting. And you are even able to feel a twinge of envy for Dahl, as he guides his skiff (your skiff, too, at least for the morning) out into the vastness of Superior.

The view is worth a paycheck all by itself. The sun skipping across the waters of Lake Superior illuminates the rocks and waves and sky in a way that makes the whole scene thoroughly glow, incandescent and gleaming. Like many other vantage points on the lake, the view of Knife Island at dawn is primordial—it's easy to imagine that nothing else exists by the water but the birds and the rocks and the fish. More than that, it's hard to imagine that you'll have to return to shore again. Time slows down and stops with the lapping of the lake. Of course, had we gone out on a blustery fall day, it would have been a different experience entirely. Dahl's low-to-the-water skiff is a perfect instrument for the lake to express itself through, whatever its mood may be. I say an inward prayer of thanks that we chanced our way out onto the lake when its mood was mellow.

As we emerged from the shelter of the shoreline, we felt hundreds of eyes upon us. The gulls and cormorants on Knife Island dot the rocks and toothpick-like trees, watching us make our way out onto the water. "I always feel sorry for those little ones,

Curious gulls often follow commercial fisherman Steve Dahl as he harvests herring from his nets.

hanging out up there in those storms, just getting blasted," he says, looking at the birds. "Some of the sport [fishing] guys hate 'em. They're fish eaters."

Dahl, who holds a master's degree in Scandinavian languages and literature and works a sideline profession of crafting musical instruments, is one of twenty-five commercial fishermen working the North Shore. In his mind, there should be more, and they should have the opportunity to fish lake trout as well as lake herring, but restrictive policies of the Minnesota Department of Natural Resources (DNR) prevent it. "The herring stocks are real solid," says Dahl, as we motor out to the first of his nets. "Everything is very political. This local food movement has given us political strength."

The battle that Dahl refers to is the fight against the DNR to expand fishing on the North Shore, to bring new blood into the industry, and to widen the availability of one of the lake's great resources. "There's a terrible rift between the North Shore and St. Paul," he says. "An example of that is lake trout."

Dahl recalls an era when the lake and its fish were in much rougher shape. "The lake was an absolute mess, forty or so years ago. Lamprey, pollution . . . So the DNR came and said, 'We've got to shut down the lake trout [for commercial fishing] and get the population rehabilitated. You'll be the first ones to get back to fishing them.'

"Four to five years ago, we said [to the DNR], 'Come on, we should get some lake trout.' We crafted a plan: three thousand for Minnesota 2 [one of the regions of the lake along the shore], two thousand for Minnesota 3, none for me because of the sport fishing. . . . We crafted a ten-year master plan, took it down to the state, and [the legislature] rejected it. So we were livid."

A STRUGGLE FOR THE FUTURE OF LAKE SUPERIOR FISHING

On the DNR side of things, though, there is a fragile momentum to be preserved. While the health of the herring and lake trout populations has improved in recent years, it's not invulnerable to predation by humans or to future, unforeseen environmental crises such as invasive species.

Tom Hrabik, an associate professor of biology at the University of Minnesota Duluth, coordinates the surveys that gauge the health, numbers, and interrelationships of Lake Superior fish species. He agrees that lake fish numbers in general, and

Nearby Knife Island at sunrise.

lake herring numbers in particular, are healthy from a historical perspective, but he points out that one particularly healthy "class" of fish (that of 2003) is providing a large share of the herring being caught at the moment. Until that class is supplemented by another large group of adult herring, any increase in fishing licenses or limits could result in pressure on the population that could cause an unforeseen drop in numbers.

"It's a conservative fishery," said Hrabik, acknowledging that when forced to choose, the management style favors the overall population of fish over increasing the number of fishermen. "But until the lake herring pull off recruitment events and increase substantially in numbers, the way [fisheries supervisor] Don [Schreiner] is doing it seems to be the most prudent way to go."

Hrabik further explained that if the numbers of licenses or species fished were expanded too early, the populations might collapse and put the agency in the position to take licenses away from fishermen, which would be disastrous to the newly established members of the profession. Dahl's job, of course, is not all politics. Some of it is gauging the mood of the lake. He has nets to watch and protect, a living to make, and a life to safeguard against the dangers of the lake.

Today, thankfully, the weather as we head out onto Superior could hardly be more perfect: sunny, a light breeze, relative warmth. But during peak herring season (October and November of each year) the lake can turn vicious and unpredictable. At that point, it's each fisherman's intuition and experience in a game of chance against the lake and its ever-shifting moods. "Yeah, you get a feel for it," says Dahl over the putter of the outboard motor. "Sometimes you don't even want to listen to the marine forecast, all gloom and doom. You just have to go outside and look at it and figure out if you can do it or not." Dahl recalls the era before motorized skiffs: "The old timers got killed by the northwest wind, when they had sail and oars, and they blow out into the middle of the lake," he says. "They'd get overwhelmed or freeze to death."

Mid-October through November is the herring run—40 percent of Dahl's income comes from that five weeks. He can back split seventy pounds of fish every fifteen minutes, cleaning and inspecting the valuable roe as he goes. Dahl sells most of his catch in Knife River. Some goes to Russ Kendall's, where it's smoked. The rest is shipped out, but high local demand keeps most of it from going any farther than Two Harbors. "We're getting past that generational thing where I go 'herring,' and people go 'Uuugh.'" (Pickled herring takes at least some of the blame for this.) Locally, herring is the key component in fish cakes. When done well, they're sublime, akin to and on par with crab cakes in terms of simplicity and flavor impact. Inspired by Scandinavian cuisine, fish cakes are sautéed patties of ground fish mixed with eggs and spices. Since they are generally considered home cooking, you're lucky if you find them on a restaurant menu, although the Satellite's Country Inn on Highway 61 near Taconite Harbor is locally famous for their sterling rendition of the dish.

After being dressed and sold, the fish caught near Knife Island travel far and wide. "They utilize some at the Scenic Café," says Dahl, referring to one of the North Shore's haute cuisine hot spots, "but most of it goes to Sweden. The Swedes, they sample everything they buy. It's probably distributed to Norway, and Finland and Northern Germans."

Dahl would like to see more of his fish eaten close to home, but American eating habits just aren't there yet. "I worked in Norway, and breakfast was a slice of bread, butter, and cod roe on it. It's normal!" he insists. "It's funny that the whole Scandinavian thing with fish has been lost. Andreas Viestad, this Norwegian who has cookbooks out, he talked about a rakfisk which is a fermented fish. . . . Americans are like, 'Oh, God!' But it's a delicacy."

LOCAL FOOD, LOCAL FISH

Fishing is part of a bigger picture for Dahl: a need to return to local food and to understanding the origins of what you eat. "My wife was one of a half a dozen people to start a locavore group," says Dahl. "What's interesting is that one woman says that right after World War II, 49 percent of the households in America had gardens, and now it's 1 percent. . . . it's slowly inching back, but how sad! It's convenience."

Dahl is working the nets, now, pulling the wet threads over the drum mounted on the front of his skiff. The net—all five hundred feet long and sixteen feet deep of it—stays in position as Dahl pulls on it, essentially tugging the boat through the water from one end of the net to the other. In the process, he finds herring caught in the net, each a pound or two in weight, not much bigger. Dahl twists them dexterously from the net and tosses them onto plastic fish boxes of ice in the middle of the boat. When the herring run is on and the nets are full, the center of Dahl's skiff will contain a wall of boxes full of herring, and walking from the fore to the aft of the boat means clambering over the boxes that block his way, roiling waters be damned.

It's a long way from the classroom, a place where Dahl could have easily ended up with his interest in Scandinavian languages and literature. But he says, "I didn't want to be in a university setting anymore."

"I've walked both worlds, and there's this rift between the academic and the real," he says. "I know that sociology started out of rural sociology at Wisconsin—there's that connection. . . . The DNR guys can be so frustrating, because we [the fishermen] know nothing. They will not incorporate what we know because it has to be the scientific method . . . come on, guys!"

That's not to say he isn't putting plenty of mental energy into his current job, which requires, among other things, anticipating when and where the fish will be and whether the lake will allow him to harvest them. "To fish," he says, "you have to have hope, and you have to have theories."

While herring are Dahl's bread and butter, and lake trout are high on his wish list, he's also fond of menominee, or round whitefish. He's hoping to get a permit to fish them. "They're more herring sized, they're brown, and they're very good eating," he says. "They're mellow. If I can get this permit, Scott [Graden] would be so happy at Scenic. And Kendall's . . . Gordy says we'd be able to sell them like crazy."

Less sexy but plenty delicious are the burbot, also known as eelpout or lawyerfish. "I used to get burbot when I fished out of Duluth. It's like catfish—you have to skin it," he says. "I'd give it to friends and not tell them what it was. I'd take a bite-sized chunk and dip it in butter, and they'd say, 'It tastes like lobster!' It's disregarded . . . people catch little lawyers in lakes and throw 'em on the ice."

"It's a PR thing," he adds. "I stopped calling them lawyers. You can also call it Lake Superior cod."

As for the future of his profession, Dahl is hopeful. If young people are allowed to fish the lake and support their families with their catches, and new restaurants are able to take herring and lake trout in numbers sufficient to build local appreciation for the fish, the impact could be significant, both in terms of economics and in terms of giving more Minnesotans a direct stake in the lake and its bounty.

For every position in the area's DNR-mandated two-year fishing apprentice program, Dahl says, there are three to five interested applicants—his craft isn't dying out so much as it's evolving. Dahl points to his own apprentice, Jason, as an example of the direction things are going: college educated, with no family background in fishing, and passionate about local organic food. "I might be pathologically optimistic, but I think he represents what's happening," says Dahl.

We pull back up to the shore. The morning is full-fledged at this point, the dramatic shadows and highlights of dawn washing out into the golden glow of late summer. We have a postfishing date to get breakfast at the Vanilla Bean Café in Two Harbors, where I will calm my shaky nerves with hot coffee and the café's "Scandinavian breakfast"—caramel pecan bread French toast covered with a citrus-infused batter, drizzled with burnt sugar caramel sauce, and served with applewood-smoked bacon.

But first, we disembark from the skiff and clamber up onto the dock, where a waiting customer relieves Dahl of some of his catch, fresh as can be. Although the profession of Lake Superior fisherman seems archaic to modern eyes—a perspective not used to connecting food with its wild state and more comfortable with the packaged and processed than the fresh and raw—the future for the few commercial fishermen working the North Shore seems bright, particularly as markets and fish quotas catch up to account for the flourishing supply and increasing demand. "I cannot keep up with my market," says Dahl.

Dahl's fish can be found at markets and restaurants on the North Shore and, occasionally, in the Twin Cities.

THE ART OF FARMING A ROCKY HILL

ROUND RIVER FARM, FINLAND

We start out our conversation with David and Lisa Abazs by looking at a household convenience that is nothing more than a metal box attached to a hole in their wall. "This is our zero-energy fridge, it's for the winter, six months," says David. "It holds food right at freezing." It's a simple enough idea: during the winter, cold air is more than an annoying, uncomfortable impediment—it's a natural resource. If you can harvest it, you can profit from an otherwise unpleasant situation.

That attitude—making the best of whatever resources happen to be on hand—exemplifies what makes Round River Farm such an interesting place to visit. This

David Abazs, co-owner of Round River Farm in Finland, explains his farming philosophy in front of a hoop house.

fifty-two-acre property at fifteen hundred feet above sea level is like a theme park of the possibilities inherent in living off the grid in a wild place near the lake. Most of the land is rocky, woodsy, and wild. Only about three acres are under active cultivation, with another three or so set up as pasture.

Just getting to the farm is a minor adventure. The road off the highway fades quickly into a couple of tire ruts surrounded by undergrowth, and you have to drive at a crawl back into the woods for what seems like miles before you arrive at the property. Once you're there, you're struck by the rambling but purposeful appearance of the sprawling compound. Everywhere you look, there's a project, and in this warm summer period, there's also life: vegetables, berries, chickens, trees, rhubarb, you name it. The place is dense with biomass and teems with energy.

Walking the paths that run through the Abazses' compound—for it really is a compound, a collection of outbuildings and a sauna, greenhouses and garden beds, a Wiffle ball field and tree after tall tree—it's not hard to see the appeal of this lifestyle. Isolated but not, the farm is a place of solitude and self-reliance but also a gathering place—a place where people come together to play and eat, and where food is grown to feed both the North Shore generally and the Abazs family in particular. It's a place where people have worked out a complex but ultimately sustainable agreement with nature: "We'll tame parts of you, and you'll make parts of us a little more wild. We'll be a collection of buildings and bramble, paths and wilderness, cultivated plants and local flora, and everything will rub shoulders and get by." How marvelous it would be to put a hundred Round River Farms together somewhere, all their paths intertwining, their vegetable beds and greenhouses intermingled, their Wiffle ball fields and football fields tucked away into the thick green woods that cover the community like a green jacket in the summer and a snow-flocked gazebo in the winter.

As we talk with the Abazses, we munch on dried blueberries and crunchy dried kale, products of the local landscape processed through the dehydrating power of the sun. David, who grew up on Long Island, New York, tells us that he got the idea of being a farmer when he was young—very young. "When I was seven, I saw a documentary about the Amish, and I told my dad, when I grow up I want to farm like that," he says. "It was the simple, horse-powered, communal system that was depicted. Basically I've been pursuing that ever since. I went to a college that had an agriculture farm on it, Warren Wilson College in North Carolina. And so then, basically, I was looking for a farm wife."

"Which, of course, growing up in southern Minnesota is all I could ever imagine being," says Lisa, with a laugh. "'What do you want to be when you grow up?' 'A farm wife!' Growing up, my parents had a hobby farm, and I'd do chores at my parents' friends' houses. I had a very idealistic dream about what it would be like."

When we ask Lisa and David whether the day-to-day reality matches up with the idealistic vision, they chuckle ruefully. "I think a lot of people look at our place and think it's idyllic, but they don't see the work," says Lisa. The family bought the farm in 1977, after honeymooning at a farm in New Mexico. The original plan had been to work as caretakers on a farm in Maine and stay on in that state, but, as David tells it, "Lisa woke me up in the middle of the night and said [and here he puts on a thick Minne-soh-tah accent], 'I don't want to go to Maine! I want to go and live in Minnesota!'

"And I said, 'But you're changing all our plans!' I'd planned since I was a kid to go to Maine, and I'd studied the governors, and I'd planned to run for governor of Maine at some point, I had all these aspirations. So I said, 'I have to check it out.'"

THE FERTILITY OF HIGH, ROCKY GROUND

David went to the little adobe library near the New Mexico farm and checked out maps of Minnesota. "I said, 'Well the only place in Minnesota I'd be willing to live is Finland. It's close to the ocean, and it's over the hill so we could grow some things.'" The ocean, of course, is Lake Superior. With its vistas and access to far ports, the lake is a window on the world that keeps locals connected to something larger than their own little shop or plot of land.

Round River operates eight months a year, planting starting March 1 and finishing up around November 1. The farm works as a CSA (Community Supported Agriculture), turning a small profit ("not enough to live on," notes David, "but maybe next year it might be a third of what we'd need"). The farm originally started with livestock, and the Abazses hoped to create farmstead cheese using a herd of dairy goats. But the payback was long (ten to twelve years), and the family shifted the focus to vegetables, which have their own challenges when you're growing them on two feet of soil on bedrock. It took five years of building fertility to get the farm to a place where it could reliably grow crops.

Farm owners David and Lisa Abazs house a collection of local heritage seeds in their "seed sanctuary."

The crops are only part of what the Abazses grow at Round River. Much of their time and energy goes toward planting and harvesting knowledge. Lisa works part-time as a teacher, and David does research on local food systems for the University of Minnesota. When we spoke to him, he was working on a twelve-month fellowship. "The only way to make money farming is to do it enough to talk about it," he says. "Or you grow something illegal. Either one of those."

The essential heart of David's research is investigating the food needs and capacities of his region: "Basically, from Duluth take a seventy-five-mile radius, and then include the entire county [of St. Louis], because of all the statistics." His goal was to determine whether this area had enough fertile land to grow food for all of its people. He began by defining the region and surveying its people and its land.

The University of Minnesota saw enough promise in David's research to formalize his findings and support his work with funding and high-tech maps that blended cartography, statistics, and the use of databases. When David looked at his region (population 479,500, including fifteen counties in Minnesota and Wisconsin), he found that 1.69 million acres have average or better fertility, throwing out acres that could, in fact, be farmed but are less than desirable. "It's a very conservative base—this farm would never be on there," notes David. "And this farm is producing more per acre than most farms in this country."

As a starting point, David researched every crop that goes into the Standard American Diet (or SAD, for short). Eighty-three percent of that diet, David found, could be produced in his region. (The other 17 percent were items, such as bananas, that just can't be grown in the winter-blasted North.) He and the university worked with a group of doctors and dieticians to see if it might be possible to develop a 100 percent local and healthy diet.

"They went through hours of work, and said, 'What if we can't do it?' And I said, 'If you have to throw in olive oil to make it work and it's a 97 percent local diet, that's OK,'" recalls David. "'The goal is healthy and local, and if you can't do it, tell us why.' They ended up coming up with a 100 percent healthy local diet they were confident in—certainly healthier than SAD."

David then figured out every crop and animal, and what would be needed to produce the food—animal feed, minerals, seeds to grow crops, bedding, housing, fertilizers, and so on. The result of his inquiry? "The question is if we don't have enough land for the food that we eat, that's an important thing to know for a region," says David. "It ended up we needed 550,000 acres to do 83 percent of the SAD diet. And 379,000 acres to do 100 percent of the local diet. So we have the carrying capacity to grow our own food. So no more excuses."

The challenge, then: creating local demand in order to jump start local supply in order to facilitate more local demand . . . and so forth. "It's a chicken and egg thing," notes David. "There's not enough profit in farming, and how do you get access to the land because it's so expensive because of tourism. How do we reach the hospitals and schools? There are a lot of things moving in the right direction, but it's going to be messy and little ugly and disturbing."

THE POWER OF THE GREENHOUSE

David cites Switzerland ("they ban all imported strawberries when Swiss strawberries are in season") as an example of how the government can lead the way for a real shift to local food. He also praised a U.S. government program to help farmers pay for greenhouses. "We used to be the only people around here with a greenhouse, and now every farm has a greenhouse," he says.

Running in parallel with their work as researchers and farmers, the Abazses have put together an unusual genetic storehouse on their farm, run through a nonprofit they call "Shalom Sanctuary." Its mission: preserving different varieties of rhubarb, a durable, fecund, nutritious, flavorful plant known around the world. David has identified 162 rhubarbs worldwide; the U.S. Department of Agriculture depository has 88, and Round River Farm has 34 of those so far. The long-term goal is ambitious: assembling the entire U.S. depository and expanding from there. "It's a lifelong process," says David. "The true gift of the diversity of a plant is probably never known until it matters."

As with everything else done on the farm, the rhubarb mission has many angles: it's about preserving knowledge but also promoting rhubarb wine. "Also," notes David, "rhubarb lowers cholesterol. So there's different potentialities with that."

We leave the cozy farmhouse kitchen and stroll among the neat rows of plants and tunnel-like greenhouses, all of which are bursting with produce—squash, Swiss chard, onions, peppers, carrots, peas, and green beans that taste sweet as sugar when plucked from the vine and eaten, among others. As we tour the grounds, we bump into things like the farm's massive solar oven ("We cook with our solar oven a lot; it gets to 350 degrees," says David), solar and wind power generators ("We're not on the grid at all"), the sauna (the first building erected by the family, built at night because of a plague of blackflies), and a Wiffle ball field David calls The Field of Dreams. "Sustainable food culture is not just doing agriculture but culture, too—we do a lot of that," says David, tossing a couple pitches my way.

There's a "chaletini" (a tiny chalet that's almost like a tree house in its dimensions but could comfortably—if cozily—sleep a couple) and also a "toiletini." "I created my own wastewater system," David explains. "It drip irrigates the greenhouse and the orchard. All our water is used, and all our excrement is compost. The water is piped from our well, we're totally separate."

The heart of the farm, though, is the greenhouses. A four-crop rotation (featuring peppers, spinach, mixed greens, and others) means that the farm's most productive acreage maximizes its possible output, and by planting water-loving plants between the greenhouses, the farm takes advantage of natural irrigation from rainfall.

A system of measurements and trials is in place to help identify the plant breeds that do best on the Abazses' land and in Finland's climate. "Every plant will be weighed," says David. "These [tomatoes] have competed well with a hybrid Monsanto bought. We're looking for eleven pounds of ripe tomatoes a plant, and the other eleven are green. We're identifying heirloom ones within that range so we can save our own seed."

When we ask David about how he and Lisa acquired the skills to put together a place like this, he laughs. "A lot of the stuff we ended up doing . . . it wasn't like, 'let's learn how to be a plumber,' or 'let's learn how to be an electrician.' It was more like, 'plumbers cost $60 an hour.'" What David and Lisa Abazs have accomplished—and are in the process of accomplishing—at Round River Farm is ambitious, to say the least. But some of the insights that they're making, documenting, and teaching—about plant breeds, and self-sustainability, and eking a living out of tough, cold, slanted soil—are likely to have a positive impact on the Lake Superior foodshed for years to come.

Round River Farm's produce can be obtained through their CSA:
www.facebook.com/RoundRiverFarm

GEORGE WILKES AND THE ANGRY TROUT

ANGRY TROUT CAFE, GRAND MARAIS

"Our theme is to tap into local food," says George Wilkes, coproprietor of the Angry Trout in Grand Marais. Wilkes has made a regional name for himself with his restaurant, which, like Round River Farm, is half economic engine and half laboratory for living, breathing, and thinking local. The region lives and breathes through the restaurant's architecture (it was originally a fish house), its site (right on the water), and its decor. From locally made stained glass art pieces to menus made from recycled purveyor boxes to handcrafted salt and pepper shakers, the Angry Trout resonates with the lake and its people.

Each table is made from a different sort of locally harvested tree, as indicated by carefully made labels. A thoughtful guest can learn the basics of local flora just by making multiple visits and keeping her eyes peeled. Wilkes can point at almost any aspect of the restaurant and highlight a local connection, whether its the food, the tables, the chairs, or the locally crafted salt and pepper shakers. "Every time we're going to buy something, we ask, 'Can we get that locally?' and you'd be surprised at how often you can."

Wilkes put together a book called *The Angry Trout Notebook.* It's half recipe book, the sort put out by any restaurant that's survived for more than ten years, but half a guide to the local purveyors, artisans, and other community members who have given the Angry Trout its look, feel, and flavor. Flip through it, and you'll meet local maple syrup producers, wild ricers, bakers, woodworkers, fishermen, and more. You'll also find the explanation for the name, written by George's wife and partner, Barb LaVigne. It was inspired by a recurring doodle created by her "trout fisherman boyfriend" that graced their correspondence—that fisherman was/is George. "It's sort of like the name of some old New England, *Moby Dick*–esque pub gone a little wrong," she adds.

"Sustainability sums it up—really trying to integrate the economics of the restaurant with an environmental ethic," says Wilkes. "And the way to do that is to build community and to make connections within the community, economically, but food-wise and ecologically as well. And socially, too. That's kind of the basis of sustainability—there's economics, environmental issues, and social issues."

For all its aspirations, the restaurant started humbly, as a sailboat ride business.

George Wilkes, owner of the Angry Trout restaurant in Grand Marais.

A local take on "fish and chips" at the Angry Trout Cafe.

In 1987, the sailboat business started selling a little food—humble stuff, hot dogs and ice cream. The addition of local fish and chips to the menu in the early 1990s was the turning point—the freshness of fish obtained right next door turned workaday pub grub into a reflection of the area's natural flavor.

"Next door" in this case is the Dockside Fish Market, a Grand Marais institution that is just one building down the water from the Angry Trout. From the Dockside's catch come the practically-still-flopping-in-the-net herring (and herring roe) that give the restaurant its signature flavor. "We have a lovely relationship with our fisherman [Harley and Shele Toftey next door]," says Wilkes. "He supplies us, and it's a great situation where the fish is very fresh. The ordering is extremely easy and convenient . . . we can watch him come in. There's no packaging."

Wilkes trained as a biologist, and taking over his parents' boat ride business wasn't part of the original plan. But the location of the Angry Trout—right on the Lake Superior shore—drew him into the business. "We realized it was a very nice location

GRILLED HERRING AND HERRING ROE APPETIZER AT ANGRY TROUT CAFE

Fish roe tends to be a mix between salty, mineral-inflected, and fishy, and its intensity varies greatly depending on type and condition. The herring roe served at Angry Trout is surprisingly delicate in flavor, its mild minerality well matched by the accompanying dill and onion sauce.

Despite its predominance in Baltic and Scandinavian countries (much of Superior's roe goes abroad to satisfy European demand), Americans haven't yet developed much of a taste for the stuff. That's a shame, because roe (a general term for fish eggs that includes caviar) is one of the most elegant ways to start a meal. Herring roe enjoyed dockside overlooking Lake Superior on a warm summer's night may be the most appropriate meal for a visitor.

Possible exception: grilled whole herring. That the herring arrive fresh at the neighboring Dockside Fish Market certainly must play a part in how delicious the fish and its eggs tend to be at Angry Trout. The grilled herring with wild rice that we tried rated a perfect ten for taste and texture, and though we hate to choose favorites, it was certainly among the three or four most life-changing things we tasted during our trips to the lake. Cold water gen-

erally leads fish to grow more slowly than their warm-water brethren (think of the lightning-fast growth rate of the tilapia, for example), but it makes for firmer flesh and, usually, a milder, sweeter flavor. We found fresh herring to be mild and sweet to the extreme, complemented by the nutty flavor of the wild rice and the slight caramelization and char imparted by the grill.

for a restaurant," he recalls. "My wife and I have always had an environmental ethic, so we want to apply that to the restaurant.

"We started planning the menu around things we could source locally," says Wilkes. "That's really been quite successful. The things that are kind of obvious—the fish has worked out quite well for us, the wild rice, we go through a lot of that . . . the things we get locally have been very successful." One of the restaurant's intriguing near misses: local crayfish. "People could just never catch enough of them," says Wilkes, ruefully. "I'm not done with that yet, we'll try again . . . there is one place where there's quite a few of them."

Wild rice in particular is a way for the restaurant to connect with the history and culture of the greater Lake Superior region. The book *Duluth: Sketches of the Past* puts wild ricing into a cultural context and illustrates its centrality to the old Ojibwa way of life:

> The greatest activity of the Ojibwa year was the gathering of wild rice, or mano-min. The autumn rice camp brought to an end the season in which people worked together in large groups. During September, manominikegisiss, or the moon of the gathering of wild rice, each family erected permanent or tempo-rary houses on the shores next to their rice fields. Family groups had specific shares of the rice fields and family ownership was seldom disputed. . . . During the three or four weeks of rice camp, wild rice was collected by "knocking" rice grains onto woven mats placed in the bottoms of canoes. It was then cured by parching over slow-burning fires, threshed by beating and treading, and win-nowed by fanning or by tossing rice and chaff in the breeze. Finished rice was then stored in caches to keep it from being eaten by animals or stolen by an enemy.

Wild rice failures were responsible for major hardships for the Lake Superior Ojibwa, and territorial disputes over wild rice fields often led to battles with warriors from the Dakota tribe.

"Just from selling wild rice and serving it, we've learned about its cultural history, and how important it is to [indigenous] people," says Wilkes. "And Barb and I have learned about how to parch it, and prepare it."

A book called *The Ecology of Commerce: A Declaration of Sustainability* by Paul

Hawken served as intellectual fuel for the Angry Trout as it grew in the 1990s, and Wilkes and LaVigne actively worked to weave an ethos of sustainability—environmental, gastronomic, and economic—throughout the enterprise. From a business perspective, the approach has worked. The Angry Trout is one of the best-known and most critically acclaimed restaurants on the North Shore.

"Economically, we've been quite successful even through the last few years, because we have quite a good tourism industry here," says Wilkes. "It's quite a special little place because it's the Twin Cities' favorite place to go. We've seen some serious developmental pressures, though—second homes being built, people moving back into the woods—it's losing that sense of place, the real wildness of the area is diminishing. It's a real threat."

The menu, with its emphasis on fresh fish, wild rice, and local produce (including fruits and vegetables from Belluz Farms in Thunder Bay), is a way to fight back against that fading sense of place. The owner's self-imposed burger and soda ban—flying in the face of the old-school staples that have defined north-country tourist traps for years and are still the heart of places like Gordy's Hi-Hat in Cloquet—was a point of pride.

In 2011, the Angry Trout added burgers to its menu—but on Wilkes's terms. The burgers are made from pasture-raised meat from Thousand Hills of Cannon Falls, Minnesota. The initial resistance to serving mass-marketed soda products has persisted, and customers at the restaurant can choose from an array of house-made sodas, mixed with flavors like cherry, vanilla, lemon-lime, strawberry, and even diet cola.

"It's just so nice not to give your money to Coke or Pepsi," Wilkes says. "Our favorite we make is a maple syrup soda. We just use carbonated water, ice, and maple syrup. That's the best from a sustainability point of view—it's locally made and nothing but syrup and water."

Angry Trout Cafe, 408 Highway 61, Grand Marais, 218-387-1265.
www.angrytroutcafe.com

OTHER EXPERIENCES ALONG MINNESOTA'S NORTH SHORE

JJ ASTOR RESTAURANT AND LOUNGE

505 West Superior Street, Duluth, at the Radisson Hotel. www.jjastorrestaurant.com

Perched atop the Radisson Hotel in Duluth and named for a legendary fur magnate, JJ Astor Restaurant and Lounge is both of the North Shore and deliberately accessible to business travelers in search of comfort. Its menu includes some nice local flourishes (a delicious fry bread–based appetizer featuring prosciutto, figs, and balsamic vinegar, and pecan-crusted walleye) and some international dishes such as sea scallops and osso bucco. Lake Superior Brewing beers are available on draft, and, most critically, the entire restaurant rotates slowly, turning 360 degrees over the course of an hour, allowing views of the harbor, downtown Duluth, and the hills in which the town is situated.

TYCOONS, THE ZENITH ALEHOUSE

132 East Superior Street, Duluth. www.tycoonsalehouse.com

Hearty pub grub (including fish from Northern Waters) and Fitger's beer make Tycoons a worthy consideration for a Duluth-based meal, but its the interior decor that makes it a must-see. This newly opened bar and eatery was originally built as Duluth's city council building and jail, and the space has an old-fashioned majesty to it. The basement rathskeller (not yet open) should add a charming German beer–hall dimension to the spot that will make it a serious local draw.

LAKE SUPERIOR BREWING

2711 West Superior Street, Duluth. www.lakesuperiorbrewing.com

"I think being close to and named for the lake has some kind of stabilizing influence," wrote Lake Superior Brewing brewmaster Dale Kleinschmidt in an e-mail interview, when asked about the significance of his brewery's name and location. "I feel that going forward the company should incorporate the big lake experience into the business image. I think of the lake as immediately impressive, unique, interesting, enjoyable, lasting and an experience leaving you wanting more. All of which relate to what I would like people to relate to LSB."

Lake Superior Brewing is a powerful force on the North Shore, and its reach descends into the Twin Cities and the south shore of the lake. Tours are available upon request and are, along with eating at Fitger's, a good way to connect with local craft brew. Its Kayak Kolsch is one of the most perfectly matched craft beer flavors available on the shores of Superior—its clean, crisp, pure flavor profile echoes the visual impact of the lake itself.

NEW SCENIC CAFÉ

5461 North Shore Drive, Duluth. www.sceniccafe.com

Located squarely right across scenic North Shore Drive from the shore of the lake, the New Scenic Café offers one of the most intimate gastronomic communions with the water in the Duluth–Superior area. The menu changes frequently, and on its best nights, New Scenic presents subtle snapshots of local food, reflecting farm, forage, and fish. On its worst, it's an adequate trip to a hotel bistro doing California-inspired dishes. The raspberry rhubarb pie, when available, is a must-eat. Customers ought to order their own piece or prepare for silverware-based warfare.

VANILLA BEAN CAFÉ

812 7th Avenue (Highway 61), Two Harbors. www.thevanillabean.com

The Vanilla Bean Café does dinner throughout the tourist high season, but breakfast is the star of the show at this cozy, casual spot. Buttermilk pancakes, crepes, Swedish pancakes, and a creamy wild rice porridge are highlights of the sweet side of the menu, while plate-sized oven-baked omelets are the house specialty on the savory end of things. If you've worked up an appetite by swimming, canoeing, biking, or hiking, the Vanilla Bean is one of the most reliable ways to undo any caloric good you might have accomplished.

RUSTIC INN CAFE

2773 Highway 61, Castle Danger. www.therusticinncafe.com

The Rustic Inn operates as a restaurant and gift shop, but the homemade pie is the core of its business, at least from a visiting gourmet's perspective. The menu is dominated by pub grub and some unremarkable heavier options (roasted sirloin, Alaskan king salmon, Cajun sausage pasta). Eat light and save room for pie, including the restaurant's notorious apple caramel pecan pie, a gooey explosion of sweetness, tartness, and crunchiness.

The birth of the Castle Danger Brewery in 2011 provides added appeal to the Rustic Inn for beer lovers. Castle Danger's brews tend to be light and lively, suited to north-country outdoor adventures. The brewery's corn-, honey-, and malt-kissed Castle Cream Ale, in particular, makes for effortless summer sipping. The brewery is situated at Castle Haven Cabins, a family resort also owned by brewers Clint and Jamie MacFarlane.

SATELLITE'S COUNTRY INN

9346 Highway 61, Schroeder

This small, rustic place doesn't look like much from the outside, but it's one of the least pretentious and tastiest spots to stop on the North Shore. A meal of firm, brightly flavored, house-made herring fish cakes with house-made tartar sauce followed by pie is the main attraction at Satellite's Country Inn in Schroeder. You can even order your fish-cake dinner as a surf and turf—the Moo Fin Burger puts the cake atop a beef patty.

DOCKSIDE FISH MARKET

418 Highway 61, Grand Marais. www.docksidefishmarket.com

Located next door to the Angry Trout, the Dockside Fish Market offers some of the freshest herring and herring roe available on the lake, courtesy of owners Harley and Shele Toftey. They fish the lake as well as manage their humble but charming restaurant/deli.

THE NANIBOUJOU LODGE

20 Naniboujou Trail, Grand Marais.
www.naniboujou.com

The ceiling at the Naniboujou Lodge is one of the most beautiful architectural sights around the shores of Lake Superior, a riot of geometric red, orange, and black patterns and icons inspired by Cree Indian designs. Rendered by French artist Antoine Goufee, the ceiling's designs were compared to "a North Woods answer to the Sistine Chapel" by writer Tom Clifford. Tasteful grandeur and a sense of communion with the lake make this restful spot a special place in the hearts of its guests. Wild rice omelets, homemade cinnamon rolls, and homemade granola define the breakfast service; upscale burgers, fish, and steaks anchor the classic dinner menu.

The hand-painted ceiling of the Naniboujou Lodge dining room is one of its best features.

CANADIAN WATERS

THE RETURN OF EATING LOCAL

The revelry, impromptu races, and wild dancing of the North West Company's Great Rendezvous were centered in the 60-foot long Great Hall [of Fort William, near Thunder Bay]. Here the men dined on buffalo tongue and hump, smoked lake trout and whitefish, roasted venison and beaver tail, stuffed ducks and goose, topped off with rich confectioneries brought all the way from Montreal. . . . Think of it: up to two thousand visitors crowded together in this remote post at the head of Lake Superior at a time when the entire population of York— soon to become Toronto—numbered fewer than five hundred.

Barbara Chisholm and Andrea Gutsche,
Superior: Under the Shadow of the Gods

IN THE INFANCY OF CARTOGRAPHY, as humanity struggled to create maps that were surrounded by voids of unexplored territory, mapmakers would famously fall back on mythical monsters ("Here be dragons") as a way to signify the unknown. For many American food lovers, the world may as well end at the Canadian border; Sault Ste. Marie and Thunder Bay could be rendered with a manticore and a griffin, respectively, for all the cross-border gastronomic interchange that takes place.

Go north across that invisible line, and things really do change. Canadian red tape keeps the province of Ontario from spawning and supporting the robust and booming craft beer and artisan cheese industries that make Minnesota, Wisconsin, and Michigan increasingly vibrant destinations for passionate eaters and beer fans. Travelers who stick to the main highway will find that much of the food on the road is trucked in and charmless, essentially the same mass-market, straight-from-frozen chow that you can get from California to Maine.

In an article titled "From Kraft to Craft: Innovation and Creativity in Ontario's Food Economy," Queen's University scholar Betsy Donald quotes from a 1957 radio interview with Kentucky Fried Chicken's spokesman Colonel Sanders in which he said that "Canada had no cuisine and that there wasn't one dish he particularly enjoyed on his trips across Canada." In recent years, Ontario has been fighting a reputation for "bland food" by pushing policy changes to support locally grown and craft foods. Donald also cites a 2008 report that documents that while the larger food sector in the province has grown only 2 to 3 percent annually, Ontario's creative food economy

Kakabeka Falls is a popular attraction for visitors to Thunder Bay.

subsector (defined as "local, organic, specialty, and/or ethnic foods") has grown at a much faster rate, between 15 percent and 25 percent per year.

After years of evolution, the food economy has begun to pivot from efficiency and centralization to a realization of the importance and value of a sense of place—and of the positive economic impact the decentralized, local production of food can have on a finished artisan product.

In 2012, Premier Dalton McGuinty put forth the Local Food Act, pushing to put more Ontario-grown produce in grocery stores, as well as hospitals, schools, and other institutions. "If every one of our families were to spend $10 more every week on Ontario foods, that would have a $2.4 billion impact on the economy and create 10,000 jobs," McGuinty said in a *Toronto Star* interview. "We're buying the food anyway right now, for example, in our public institutions. It's just a matter of ensuring that we're using our purchasing power to support local agriculture."

While the provincial government seeks to promote new habits of eating locally, some sparks of beauty from the past smolder onward, reminding guests of a simpler, purer era of eating. The craft resurgence is underpinned by food traditions that have soldiered through the culinary Dark Ages in Canada and are now emerging into a climate more welcoming of the homemade and regional. Finnish bakeries and restaurants in Thunder Bay balance sweetness and spice with a sophisticated Old World sense of restraint. Smoked fish offered in little shops and farmers markets are as skillfully made as any in the world. Green shoots of new culinary life are beginning to peek out from the fertile soil of Thunder Bay as residents reconnect with local produce, fine cooking techniques, and the bounty of Lake Superior. In twenty years, Thunder Bay could be giving Duluth–Superior a culinary run for its money, and that time could be halved if the provincial government unfetters and supports those who would develop small-scale artisan food.

While traveling through the city, we picked up a copy of the local alt-weekly (appropriately enough, it's called the *Walleye*) and read a feature on the "Thunder Bay Burger," a "truly local burger" using cheese, meat, buns, and produce from local purveyors, who were called out by their name and Web site. The passion is there.

The history of the Thunder Bay area—as home to people of the Anishinaabe, or Ojibwa, First Nation, and then, after white settlement, as a center of forestry and paper milling—remains in evidence, but its future as a center of higher learning and

Local produce is a common sight at the Thunder Bay Country Market.

medical center is snapping into focus as new construction remakes the city. Thai, Japanese, and Indian restaurants have joined a mix of Italian and Finnish options that have roots in the area's ethnic bedrock, and farmers markets and local produce initiatives are increasingly contributing to the offerings of higher-end restaurants.

Farther to the east, past the vast and starkly beautiful northern shore of the lake, visitors can find tired relics of the region's past in the run-down rust-belt town of Sault Ste. Marie, Ontario, a city driven by chain restaurants and fast food in direct contrast to the small but lively resurgence of local food just across the locks in Sault Ste. Marie, Michigan. But visitors who keep their eyes peeled as they make their journey around the northern part of the lake can find some culinary gems that are special to this part of Ontario and reflect access to nearly limitless clean water and pristine natural surroundings. For the observant traveler, the Canadian side of the lake reveals some lovely treasures.

THUNDER BAY: SPARKS OF THE OLD

Before you can taste the treasures of Thunder Bay, you have to crack the tough shell of this hard-working industrial town by the lake. In 1970, Thunder Bay was created by the union of two existing communities, Fort William and Port Arthur. (A naming referendum saw "Lakehead" and "The Lakehead" splitting much of the vote, throwing the victory to the less-popular name of "Thunder Bay," which triumphed by a mere 500 votes.) This union of cities left an industrial intercity zone anchored by a shopping mall, which makes for a disconcerting experience for the first-time visitor, who might expect, in its place, a plaza, statehouse, or other imposingly beautiful piece of public architecture. Passing out of the downtown district of Fort William, you move north into a collection of warehouses, industrial buildings, and other edge-of-city commercial enterprises (surprisingly studded by the odd fine-dining restaurant), until you reach the downtown district of Port Arthur.

Largely invisible to casual observers, noteworthy and strengthening strands of local food culture are starting to bring the dining scene to life. In the walkable Bay-Algoma district in old Port Arthur, its extensive Finnish heritage provides a lovely and savory experience for visitors. Gift shops mingle with restaurants and old Finnish bakeries, like Harri Bakery on Algoma Street. Owned by Finnish immigrant Harri Kurtti, Harri Bakery is known for its cookies and bread, simple products made in a European tradition that values taste, restraint, and balance over bushels of sugar and icing. The shop's sour rye bread, coffee bread, ginger cookies, and Christmas prune stars are among its best sellers.

"We're much gentler with the sugar, and less colors even," says Kurtti. "We've been educated to use color more carefully. People like it, they like the not-too-sweet stuff. I also make no doughnuts, we've got so many doughnut places."

Kurtti himself couldn't be more suited to his place and occupation. As he peeks around his custom shelves to grasp a cookie with tongs, he is cheerful and focused, a man very much in his element and part of his community. Once upon a time your job—baker, butcher, blacksmith, farmer—was an immutable part of your identity and with you forever. While both a blessing and a curse, your job made you feel comfortable and defined in an ever-changing world. Now, people jump from city to city and office to office every few years, redefining themselves with training and résumés

PERSIAN DOUGHNUTS IN THUNDER BAY

The Persian Man, 899 Tungsten Street, Thunder Bay

Stop just about anywhere that food is sold in Thunder Bay, and you'll have a chance to pick up a Persian, a local delicacy unique to the region. This oval sweet roll boasts a sweet pink icing, very often raspberry or strawberry, although we tried and particularly liked the blueberry variety as well. There's no known link between the Persian and the nation of Persia (known in modern times as Iran); locals, including Joe Nucci of Nucci Bake-a-Deli at The Persian Man, say that the doughnut was named for U.S. General John Pershing. The Persian Man bakery is a fine place for your first Persian experience, but local grocery stores, gas stations, and bakeries all offer their own takes on the staple food.

and degrees, not shoes or bottles of wine or loaves of bread. To meet a brewer or a fisherman or a baker like Kurtti is to meet someone comfortable in his own skin, assured a place in the community by virtue of having chosen a way to make a living that is instantly understandable and self-evidently valuable. Take a deep breath in Kurtti's shop, smell the sugar and cardamom and fruit, and you know why what he does is important.

"I started it in 1985," recalls Kurtti. "I was working for someone else, but people were asking, when are you going to start your own store? I was twenty-three when I came over from Finland. It was just me, just myself—first time flying. There was a Finnish bakery that was looking for a worker, and that was me. My education in Finland was in baking." Kurtti's two-year trade school education and apprenticeship in baking in Finland left him firmly grounded in his country's traditions, something that pleases his customers.

"I have added hardly anything more—I have kept everything the same," says Kurtti. "I'd say my customers are 30 percent Finns, and the rest non-Finns—ethnic Italians, and so on. And that map is of customers who have come to me from all over the world."

The Finland connection was critical to Kurtti's bootstrapping his way into the business. When he founded the shop, he recalls, "I went to a big bank and asked for money and they said 'hmm, we don't really . . . come and talk to us later.' But then I went to

Finnish immigrant Harri Kurtti is owner of Harri Bakery in Thunder Bay.

my local Finnish credit union . . . no problem! The first day I opened, I had more flowers in my store than baking, I sold out . . . I thought, I should start a flower shop! I was surprised how easy it was to start the business."

We asked Kurtti if he had any plans to jump on board the current trends in baking: cupcakes, French macarons, and so forth. "No!" exclaims Kurtti, with mock outrage. "Leave that for someone else! No chance!"

Baking is a notoriously tough grind, but when we asked Kurtti whether he enjoyed his work, his face lit up. "I do! That's the thing! I get up early in the morning, quarter to three in the morning . . . I have my weekends off, and I love to do it, the baking, by hand . . . and it gives me my daily bread. It gives me a lot of satisfaction."

As we left Kurtti's shop, he pressed a loaf of cardamom raisin coffee bread into our arms, and we left, grateful and somewhat surprised. The next six hours of reporting, as it turns out, were a blur of activity that offered no time to stop and eat, and we found ourselves sustained and revived by that bread. Mildly sweet and beautifully spiced, it was a perfect complement to the Tim Hortons coffee that we gulped down as we drove to and from local farms and restaurants.

Harri Bakery, 223 Algoma South, Thunder Bay, 807-344-8588

FINLAND ON THE LAKE

THE FISH SHOP, THUNDER BAY

Finland manifests itself in more than baked goods—the Finnish tradition of smoked fish is alive and well at The Fish Shop, just east of Thunder Bay on the Trans-Canada Highway. Owner Liisa Karkkainen and her family have been perched on the edge of the lake since 1969, and while her establishment may now have the feel of a modern gift shop and working fish smokery, it was once just a trailer in the "bush," as the wilderness is known on this side of the border. "[My parents] were Finns, from Finland," says Karkkainen, "so they knew about fishing, and bush work, and farming, agrarian society . . . From there, things have just taken on a life of their own."

The largest wave of Finnish immigration into Canada occurred between 1900 and the start of World War I, largely due to a diminishing economic and political situation for working-class families in Finland. Canada was able to offer a variety of jobs in the logging and mining industries, and the similarity in climate to Finland was desirable for Finnish immigrants looking for farmable land. The Canadian "bush" country would be considered wild and rugged to almost anyone in Europe, but to Finns it felt similar to their own land of lakes and trees.

After World War I, the United States put heavy restrictions on immigration, and Canada became an even more desirable location for Finnish immigration. According to the available census data, Canadians of Finnish origin numbered 15,497 by 1911, 43,885 by 1931, and 59,346 by 1961. Currently, Thunder Bay has the largest Finnish population outside of Scandinavia.

That population is the core of The Fish Shop's customer base. While the shop has expanded to include local amethyst specimens and cedar garden furniture, Finnish-style smoked fish is the core of the shop's business and identity. The fish is delicately smoked to achieve a luminous, metallic color, as though each piece was hand brushed with gold. "The way we smoke fish is the same way they've been doing it for seven hundred years in Finland," says Karkkainen. "So there's no chemicals, nitrates, color, liquid smoke."

"The things that are in style now—recycling, eating local food, supporting your local business, all this—like that's what Finn culture has always been about," she

Liisa Karkkainen, owner of The Fish Shop in Thunder Bay, serves up what her shop does best.

SMOKED FISH
price per pound

HERRING 6⁸⁰
WHITEFISH 6⁸⁰
TROUT 6⁸⁰
SALMON - $14.⁵⁰
TROUT FILLET - $10 -
*PICKEREL - $16.⁹⁵

TANDOORI NUGGETS 8⁵⁰/6oz
MAPLE CANDIED NUGGETS 1.⁴⁰oz
INDIAN CANDY 8⁵⁰/6oz
JERKY 8⁵⁰/6oz

LOX 12⁵⁰/7oz
KIPPERS 3⁵⁰ pkg

FRESH DRESSED
price per pound

LAKE TROUT 5⁵⁰ → WHITEFISH
SALMON 9⁹⁶   PICKEREL 9⁹⁵
HERRING 3⁵⁰   NORTH PIKE 3⁴⁰

FRESH FILLET
price per pound

PICKEREL 12⁹⁵   HADDOCK 9⁹⁵
LAKE TROUT 8⁷⁵   COD 8⁷⁵
WHITEFISH 8⁷⁵
SALMON 14⁹⁵   NORTH PIKE 8⁷⁵

PAY DIRECT

Karkkainen's smoked fish is readily available at The Fish Shop and has been prepared the same way for generations.

adds. "We've always said, how stupid to go to the grocery store and buy a fish from China when you can get the best right here, hey? We've got our ideas all mixed up."

For Karkkainen, the lake is a sacred place, a unique resource that must be protected and honored. She puts it in context: "This is the last freshwater fishery in the world that's sustainable in grade A condition—and the water, you can take a cup and drink it anywhere.

"Even around here, some people will discount Lake Superior—they'll say, 'I'd never eat a fish from Lake Superior.' They're all big on inland lakes, from shallow, warm water. And I belong to Slow Food. We went in 2006 to Italy, to Terra Madre to the big convention. We were the only fish people in all of Canada invited to go because of the way we smoke the fish, and we're dealing with third- and fourth-generation commercial fishermen, who are really rough and tough—they're like the farmers on the water."

Liisa's uncle drowned in 1978 while fishing the lake, so she's all too aware of the challenges of harvesting its bounty. "It's very dangerous work, but it's so important to the lake. And when you go to places like Egypt and Asia where it's people on top of people, and then you come here where we have all this bush and land, and no smog . . . like this is so perfect, and the fish here, to have them," she says.

"That's why it drives me crazy when people would rather go to the grocery store and pay $2.99 for that slab of fish from China. When I went to Terra Madre, and I talked to fishermen from around the world . . . their fisheries are doomed, doomed. And you talk about mercury, there's no mercury here. In the oceans, the main things are the PCPs and the flame retardants, which you can't police. . . . But the lake, you've got Canadians on one side and Americans on the other, and I think the Americans are even more vigilant about protecting it. I felt really empowered after I went there."

The Fish Shop works with two different commercial fishermen, who net fish and bring it to the shop direct by truck. The shop hires locals (mostly Finns, she notes). As for their wares, Karkkainen says the shop trades in "herring, whitefish, pike, and we import salmon from Vancouver Island—wild Canadian salmon, we don't have no China fish here. And that's a small thing. Whitefish is number one, that's king, for sure."

The smoking is a three-day process. A mild sea-salt brine is applied to a fish that has been frozen for three months; freezing breaks down the fish's cellular structure, Karkkainen notes, which makes it more accepting of the brine. The fish are thawed in cold water, brined, and then hung in the smoker. A typical week for the shop might produce a ton of smoked fish, using green alder wood. "That's the only thing my mom said was correct," Karkkainen says. "Alder's everywhere, and it's scrap wood—most people are happy to have us take it away. Green, whole alder—not chipped, not dried, only alder.

"It keeps the fish moist, and mild, and they look like they're painted gold," says Karkkainen, picking up some of her product and showing it off for the camera. "It's

Frozen fish is cut by hand at The Fish Shop.

awesome. There's no black sooty look, and there's no carcinogenic properties . . . it's perfect."

The Fish Shop is, in short, the kind of shop you can build a community around: rooted thoroughly in an authentic local tradition (Finnish fishing) but adapted to the modern marketplace (pizza and amethyst jewelry), producing its own lovely value-added product (smoked fish) but selling plenty of goods from the rest of the community (eggs and Finnish pasties). It is a place of both commerce and conversation, a gathering place not just for things to buy but also ideas to ponder and people to meet, either literally or through the things they have made and caught and crafted and mined. Once upon a time, the general store was the way that news was exchanged and crucial community buying and selling happened. The Fish Shop feels like the modern expression of that ideal, at once quaint and lively, a throwback that just happens to be busy and relevant.

The Fish Shop, 1960 Lakeshore Drive, McKenzie, 807-983-2214. www.thefishshop.ca

HARVESTING THE SUN

DEBRUIN'S GREENHOUSES, THUNDER BAY

With the help of technology and a great deal of persistence, beautiful tomatoes grow in Thunder Bay. Arjen DeBruin came to Canada in 1987 on a student exchange program and quickly found himself following in his brother's footsteps, marrying a Canadian and putting down roots. "My sister-in-law had a friend. 'Do you want to meet her?' 'Yeah, whatever.' Twenty years later, we've been married twenty years, and we've got four daughters. We started from scratch on this property—we bought it a year and a half later."

DeBruin walks us through one of his greenhouses, which is replete with tomato-laden vines. The interior is a riot of green and red and orange and yellow, with brilliant bursts of tomatoes climbing up and down the vines like fireworks. It feels like an organized jungle, full of fresh, earthy odor. The experience fills the senses, and relative to the emptiness of rural Ontario, it's a veritable feast. That the tomatoes themselves burst with flavor is almost an afterthought once you've walked through the rows of vines that fill the greenhouses.

Each season, DeBruin's Greenhouses produce about thirty thousand pounds of tomatoes, a mammoth operation for Thunder Bay but a small-scale producer in the bigger context of Canadian agriculture. His tomatoes are sold to about ten area restaurants, and when we talked to him in 2011, he was working on landing larger contracts with area mines and universities.

As we enter the greenhouse and inhale the powerful scents of tomatoes and basil, we exclaim, involuntarily, "The place is like a cathedral of produce." "That's what everybody says when they come in here," DeBruin says. "They never really thought that we could have stuff like that here [in Thunder Bay]."

As it turns out, despite its long, cold winters, Thunder Bay is the sunniest city in Ontario. "If you're going to set up greenhouses in Ontario, this is the best place to be," DeBruin says. "We were dealing with the cold weather in winter, but there are ways to work with that. Not the cheapest ways, but there are ways to work with that."

While it's currently not profitable for DeBruin to use his greenhouses during the middle of winter, he's rounding up funding for a pilot project to work toward year-round agriculture with minimal energy input. "People will say, 'Oh, this works at

Arjen DeBruin, owner of DeBruin's Greenhouses in Thunder Bay, beside his crop.

temperatures as low as . . . ten,'" says DeBruin. "Well, try minus eighteen. Or minus twenty-five. We're also looking for some funding to set up a pilot project on a greenhouse that'll go year-round with a minimal amount of energy input. It's going to be tricky, but my gut feeling is that we can do this. There's enough solar panels and parabolic dishes . . . It's something new, I have it on paper, it's just a matter of doing it.

"There are a lot of natives living north of Thunder Bay, and they need to be self-sufficient instead of living off of a handout. So let me design the greenhouse first, I have lots of experience, I have twenty-five years of experience, and heat conservation—it's me, I'm a tinkerer, I also have a patent out there for this [automated tomato vine lowering system]—it's the only one in the world."

The vine system allows workers to trim DeBruin's tomato vines regularly to keep them visible and concentrate the plants' energy on growing their colorful fruit, not foliage.

A "BIG-TIME" BOOM IN LOCAL FOOD

DeBruin splits his efforts fifty-fifty between bedded plants, like basil and lettuce, and his tomatoes. For the former, he harvests the plants with the roots attached, which means that the still-living plant will last much longer in the refrigerator. "The chill of the fridge will just slow everything down," he says. "Better yet, put a moist towel in the base of the bag, put it in the fridge—it's actually still growing, believe it or not. When you need it, take the roots off and take the core out of the plant, and you've got a fresh salad."

When asked if interest in local food is rising in the Thunder Bay area, DeBruin's eyes light up. "Big time," he says. "I don't even think we've reached the peak yet. There is no peak, I think.

"I'm one of the core members of the country market in town. . . . Fifteen years ago, twelve people, they started out this country market in the city of Thunder Bay. That was a tough go at the very beginning. . . . People were so used to going to Safeway and buying their produce there. There were some vegetable farms here, but they were very specialized in strawberries or pumpkins or things like that.

"People are more conscious of where their produce comes from. Our book is an open book here, and people know that we don't spray chemicals. If you see a little

MARGHERITA PIZZA AT CARIBOU

727 Hewitson Street, Thunder Bay.
www.caribourestaurant.com

DeBruin's cherry tomatoes and basil, as well as Thunder Oak's quark cheese and mozzarella, are played up on a fine, crisp wood-fired crust at Caribou Restaurant, home of some of the city's best-considered and most locally sourced eats. We liked the pizza but wound up raving about the apple crisp cheesecake, with its cinnamon spiced apples and candied ginger. Flavors of brown sugar, caramel, spice, and tart apple played elegantly across the blank canvas of a light, elegantly executed classic cheesecake. We're not sure how the restaurant did it, but the cheesecake stood up to those we've tried at reputable places in New York City.

bit of mildew on cucumber plants, we know that. That'll be there until the plant is harvested. We use all sorts of beneficial bugs."

DeBruin also hopes to incorporate livestock into his greenhouse scheme. "Beef [cattle] have a body temperature of about ninety-eight. They're actually very warm. [Another farmer] had about twenty cows in there, and it heats the greenhouse. He said in the middle of winter, 'My greenhouse does not go below fifteen degrees Celsius.' And I think, you know what? Maybe we should look into this. Of course, then your greenhouse won't smell like basil, it'll smell like cows . . ."

The business comes down to energy management, ultimately, and it's the miserly use of energy that allows DeBruin to grow tomatoes throughout much of the year. DeBruin's friend and land tenant Rob Walsh notes, "It's pretty amazing when it's February or March and it's minus ten, and you come in here, and the tomato plants are already three feet tall . . . they came in the first week of March."

DeBruin's Greenhouses, 3033 Highway 61, Thunder Bay, 807-475-7545.
www.debruinsgreenhouses.com

THE BOARS OF THUNDER BAY

NORTHERN UNIQUE, THUNDER BAY

Rob Walsh, who has been raising wild boars behind DeBruin's Greenhouses since August 2008, introduces himself matter-of-factly: "I'm a chef by trade. I've been dealing with these [wild boars] for about twelve years—buying them through different restaurants. This is the original pig, this is where all our pigs come from."

A divorce of two wild boar farmers put some stock on the market, and Walsh jumped at the chance. "It's a little bit of an awkward conversation with the wife. You're recently married, and she turns around and you've bought—well, at that time, we had 24 when we bought them," he recalls. "Currently we're running about 150. They breed really, really well. We've got enough stock on the ground that we can actually start to advertise them. The first eighteen months, everybody's asking, and I get frustrated with turning people away."

Rob Walsh, owner of Northern Unique in Thunder Bay.

Walsh's pigs take fifteen to twenty months to grow to market size. At that point, after processing, the animals weigh about 110 to 190 pounds, minus hair and guts. "From there," says Walsh, "they yield anything from 65 to 80 percent meat. Cows are more like 50 to 55 percent."

Walsh's meat isn't cheap. He sells it at about twelve dollars a pound, as opposed to about three dollars for factory pork at the store. "Yes, that pork may be three dollars a pound, but it doesn't take into account the environmental cost—water pollution, air pollution, people's health," he says. "[Big companies] own the feed companies, they own the slaughterhouses, they own the packing houses. It makes it hard. We have one local abattoir here, and if anything were to happen to it, the next closest one is in Dryden, which is four hours away."

For the high quality of his end product, he credits his pigs' feed: malt or alfalfa sprouts and dairy cow feed with a high-corn content, supplemented by restaurant tailings, extra produce from grocery stores, and leftover tomatoes from DeBruin's Greenhouses. "It's a much redder meat," he says. "It's much higher in protein. It's a much finer grain as well—the animals get a lot more exercise. They're out rooting and foraging and doing what pigs should be doing. I hate to bash the commercial pork product, but it's easy to do when they're basically just growing flesh in this restrained environment."

During the winter, Walsh is just working to keep his pigs alive, but between spring and fall, they grow quickly, losing 80 to 90 percent of their hair as the weather warms up. Walsh was selling about a pig a week when we interviewed him in 2011, marketing direct and working with local high-end restaurants like Caribou, where he used to work as sous chef. He emphasizes the local nature of what he does: local product, local processors, local abattoir, local customers. The fight, which he sees as ongoing but increasingly winnable, is convincing people to put time into their food.

"I think a lot of people just don't cook anymore," he says. "That's part of the whole local food movement. 'It has to be boneless!' I have lots and lots of pork ribs . . . it's barbecue season! But people want it *now*. 'I have eighteen minutes to get dinner on the table for four people. It has to be something quick.' People are under the illusion that tenderloin is the best . . . I've done lots of sausage with the cheeks, and you tell people that stuff and they're like 'ewwww.'"

THE VITAL IMPORTANCE OF COOKING AT HOME

Tied in with the rush toward faster, easier food is the loss of skills that once kept households humming: the ability to batch cook for the week, the pride of setting a homemade dinner out on the table, the pleasure of entertaining with food that your own hands have touched and prepared. Walsh is dedicated to the idea that his pigs can help bring locals back to an older, slower, ultimately healthier way of doing things in the kitchen. "It's trying to get people back into their kitchens and cooking again," he says. "I've been trying to get into convenience food, but my convenience food will never be as convenient as grocery store product. So, for them, it's been a learning process, and for the most part people are interested in doing it."

As Walsh's business grows, he increasingly finds it chafed by regulations. The local abattoir won't let him keep his pigs' blood, for blood sausage, despite demand for the product. "There's a lot of red tape," he says. "I'm of the frame of mind that if people want it, they should be able to get it. They're making educated decisions—everybody's big boys and girls, and if you want to go to the farmer down the road and buy a quart of unpasteurized milk, that should be your choice.

"But it's that whole trust relationship. Do you trust your neighbor more than the product on the shelf? But here, the government regulations are 'cook your chicken to 180 degrees,' you know? That's kind of frustrating. We've gone so far now, that the population as a whole needs to say, 'OK, that's enough. We can all make our own decisions if we want to.'"

Walsh sees some glaring contradictions between the sometimes exacting Canadian legal standards regulating commercial food safety and what, for example, hunters are able to do under the constraints of the law. "I'm a hunter myself, and you hear stories of people riding around in the middle of October. [They] gut-shoot a deer, drag it through the bush, and put it on the hood of their car, drive it around, bring it home, hang it in their garage, skin it, grind it, feed it to their kids—that's OK," he fumes. "That's not illegal to do that. But all of a sudden you can't buy unpasteurized milk or a pound of ground beef that hasn't gone through the local abattoir. The contradiction there—if people choose to make that decision, that should be their choice."

Walsh is close to his animals ("we interact every day"), and he has to be—he doesn't have a holding facility to force them into a vehicle to be transported for

Boars feed at
Northern Unique.

slaughter. "We have to convince them," he says. "They have to trust me enough that I will feed them on the trailer, and I sort them there. I close the doors on the ones we want to take, and off to the abattoir we go."

The expression "happy as a pig in dirt" resonates with the hogs of Northern Unique. They're vital, mischievous, curious, lively—rooting around, chasing, communicating with one another as they explore and inhabit their patch of ground. They're not docile, per se, but nor are they 100 percent wild. They regard Walsh with a friendly respect, and more than one noses up to our photographer to see who she might be and whether she might have brought them something good to eat.

The closeness he enjoys with his animals blurs the barrier between pet and food, but it's also an important part of the business. "They rub up on us when we come in the pen. We can actually pet them. They'll eat Milk-Bones. We're teaching them that humans are OK, because they're so agile and strong, if they wanted out, they would be gone. I've learned over the years, as long as they're fed well, and they have somewhere where they can hang out . . . they have to be entertained."

Much of Walsh's knowledge of pigs has come the hard way, he says, particularly from raising livestock in a sometimes bitterly cold climate. "Being in northwest Ontario, there's not a lot of research that's applicable to us. So there's been a lot of trialing and erroring—you're talking about individuals who have farmed over the last sixty years—they've learned a lot. But it's important they say what they have to say and that people listen, else we're going to rehash everything over again."

For Walsh, though, the entire process has been engaging and mind expanding. "I'd never built a barn before . . . I'd never built anything before, really!" he exclaims. "I'm learning on so many levels, it's really amazing."

Northern Unique pork is sold at the Thunder Bay Country Market on Saturdays. www.northernunique.com

AN ELIXIR FOR A COLD CLIMATE

THE GROWING SEASON JUICE COLLECTIVE, THUNDER BAY

Like much of the food around Lake Superior, Thunder Bay food tends toward the traditional, the rustic, and the meaty. Old-fashioned ideals often still reign: food tends to be greasy, salty, and stick-to-the-ribs. The Growing Season Juice Collective is everything that a cheeseburger isn't—dedicated to the fresh, the healthy, and the light, offering juices ranging from the "yin elixir" (celery, cucumber, pear, and greens) to the "liver mover" (beet, apple, carrot, and greens) and exotic fare including "vital shakes," cold seltzers, and big, beautiful salads.

Cofounder Jelena Psenicnik at The Growing Season Juice Collective in Thunder Bay.

Cofounder Jelena Psenicnik originally hails from Venezuela ("so I always had an issue with the lack of fresh juice [in Thunder Bay]") and was therefore motivated to bring a fresh-squeezed twist to the growing local food scene. "There are two of us who were very good friends for a long time, and we've traveled, and we've thought: 'Why isn't there a place that we can go to here [in Thunder Bay]?'" says Psenicnik.

"We kept talking about moving to another city, but then it occurred to us, instead of complaining, why don't we become the place that we want to be? We walked the [Bay and Algoma] neighborhood in February of 2008 and just started knocking on doors." With seventy-five dollars in the bank account and no business training, the four-woman collective opened in November 2009. In spite of the odds, and judging from its passionate following, The Growing Season has found a local niche.

"We thought it would just be this tiny place where our friends would come, maybe a few kids from the community," she recalls. "But we opened up, and it got super busy. And we were in over our heads because the demand was incredible. We had to make more tables and cram people in!

"It not just the juice, it's the idea that

there's something fresh that's available. There's something earthy about it—super simple, we just want to have some good food, some good juice. We don't even advertise. It's just a nice little place, we make all our own dressings."

The restaurant fights to be as local as possible in its sourcing, a common struggle for new locavore destinations around the lake. "It has been a challenge, just the logistics, because our demand became so high," says Psenicnik. "I'll say, 'I need six squashes every week,' and the squash lady will say, 'well . . . I have two.' I feel like Thunder Bay is trying. There are a lot of organizations—like Slow Food Thunder Bay—that are trying to set things up. Belluz Farm is supposed to be setting up a Web site so you can see all the producers."

But some of the logistics of sourcing local food are still difficult. "I can't drive a half hour every week to get food from a farm," she says. "And the carrots will come dirty as all hell, and we have to scrub them. But we try to make the effort so we can have local carrots." The end result, however, is a community increasingly energized about the possibilities of having food that is healthy and local, and a demand that is helping producers justify producing and selling more fresh produce to the Thunder Bay community.

The allure of The Growing Season is its defiance—its resolution to be different, to lead the way, to build up new pathways of eating, and sourcing, and gathering. The lightness to the space and the menu would be welcome anywhere, but here in Bay and Algoma, they are equal parts unexpected and refreshing. As a theory, it would seem unworkable, but in practice, it's a real place, filled with people, and it suggests what might be possible in this northern outpost. It is a step away from hamburgers and pizza, away from food service and frozen meals, toward something brighter. Time and time again in Thunder Bay, we got the feeling that we were exploring a metropolis that was in the process of waking up.

"I think people come in here and get pretty excited just about having healthy food," says Psenicnik. "One of our lunch dishes features lentil sprouts, and people will come in and ask, 'Well, what *are* these? How do you make those?' 'Well, we have jars in the back! We can show you!' People got so interested we even started selling [the jars]."

If Thunder Bay has been in recent decades a wasteland for the fresh and local, The Growing Season is one of the numerous green shoots of growth that indicate a renewed interest in buying local and eating more healthily. When we ate at The

Growing Season, we enjoyed the lightness and freshness of everything presented. The meal had a vibrant, almost Mediterranean feel. Psenicnik thinks that The Growing Season is not an outlier but rather a soldier for the cause of healthy eating on the vanguard of a movement.

"There are a number of things happening," says Psenicnik of the evolving local food scene. "You can see we're in the embryo stage of things, but you can see it."

The Growing Season Juice Collective, 201 Algoma Street South, Thunder Bay, 807-344-6869. www.facebook.com/pages/The-Growing-Season-Juice-Collective/181974322088

THE FLOWERS, THE BERRIES, THE BEES, AND THE TEAS

BOREAL FOREST TEAS, THUNDER BAY

After visiting the tomatoes and pigs of Thunder Bay, we headed out to another exurban part of town to tramp through the woods with Leanne Chevrette, an herbalist and a beekeeper. Chevrette is the creator of Boreal Forest Teas, made from harvested wild boreal plants and berries with organic cultivated herbs. The boreal forest (known as the taiga in Russia) is a band of northern forests typified by pines, spruces, and larches that thrive in the climate's short summers and cold winters—it's also home to the plants that Chevrette forages to make her tea blends.

As we pick our way through the property's trees, bushes, and flowers, we are struck by how lush and fertile the area seems, how busy it is with insect and bird activity—a far cry from the stark silence of winter. It's in this setting that Chevrette finds the plants that make her teas unique. "In my teas, I use probably seventeen different plants, and I have eight blends," Chevrette says. "Within those, some are wild, some are organic cultivated, and I combine the two. There's some component of wild plants in all of my teas."

Chevrette makes a point of harvesting sustainably, gently tucking away her finds in a basket that she carries with her. "I have a sense of how much you can harvest without doing harm to the plants," she says. "I have different tricks for harvesting from different parts of a patch. If you're harvesting wild plants, you have to identify

Leanne Chevrette, owner of Boreal Forest Teas in Thunder Bay.

them properly. Then you have to be knowledgeable about harvesting techniques so you ensure the population comes back. And there are ways you can harvest to increase the population of the plants, too."

All her blends, she says, are directly inspired by her experiences in the northern wilderness and her interest in boreal forest preservation. "I have my teas in fifteen different shops across Canada now," she adds. "And I have four different cafés that are serving them, so you can go in and get a cup of my tea, which is really exciting to me."

Her blends include Northern Lights (chamomile, nettle, rose hips, wild blueberries, red clover), Boreal Berry Blend (dandelion leaves, nettle, blueberries, red clover, cranberries, blueberries), Canadian Shield (peppermint, rose hips, yarrow), and several others. All have a complexity and soothing depth imparted by the variety of wild and cultivated plants that go into their creation.

What Chevrette does is a rare, precious throwback to the "gatherer" part of "hunter-gatherer" culture, which predates the rise of agriculture and fixed human settlements. It's alien to the modern world and beautiful to watch: a woman making her way through the wild boreal forest and reading it like most people read a street grid in a city, untangling the greens and browns and reds and blues and seeing instead an organized tapestry of nutrition, healing, and history. Followers of many spiritual traditions around the world would look at natural things—trees, plants, rocks, streams—and see spirits within, good or evil or some mixture of both. To watch Chevrette work is to grasp the underlying sense behind the stories, the potential for the natural world to harm or help or nourish, interpreted by a knowledgeable guide. The spirits are really there, dwelling within the plants. Whether you see them as DNA or "medicine" as the Ojibwa traditionally have, they still live and have power.

DEEP ROOTS IN THE BOREAL FOREST

Chevrette grew up in northern Ontario in a town called Timmins, about eight hours east of Thunder Bay and located in the heart of the Canadian boreal forest region. She spent much of her time in her parents' remote camp ("eleven miles up a river, no running water, no electricity, no other people—so the plants became my friends").

The connection Chevrette forged with the natural world during her childhood was nurtured and strengthened by scientific learning. She went to the University of Guelph, where she did an undergraduate degree in biology focusing on boreal forest ecology. That training led to a ten-year stint in the forest service as an ecologist. "As I was working in the realm of plant and forest ecology, I started to look a little more deeply at the plants and the plant world, and human interactions with the plants," she says.

Meanwhile, we are foraging a bit more deeply into the woods surrounding the home of Barry Tabor, a local beekeeper. Even though we're still within sight of his

Organic, wild, and local teas for sale at Boreal Forest Teas.

house, there is a wealth of useful plants, attractive flowers, and edible berries around us. To us, they're largely invisible—to Chevrette, they're plain as day. More importantly, they're critical to the way people can—or at least should—take care of themselves. "I started looking more at . . . people's use of plants and nutritional plant use, and medicinal plant use," she says. "I started doing ethnobotanical studies and worked with a number of people in the north who are really knowledgeable about plants, and it just sort of grew from there. I've been harvesting wild plants as long as I can remember.

"My grandparents used to commercially cultivate blueberries in northern Ontario, so my earliest memories were being on the land and harvesting berries and my grandmother saying, looking in my basket and saying, 'If you're not going to pick clean, don't pick it all,' which means just pick the berries and no leaves. It was a business for them."

The herbal tea business was a long-held dream for Chevrette, who found herself beset by the effort of raising young children, undertaking a graduate degree, and working full-time. But in winter 2009, things fell into place, and she was able to begin formulating her teas, working with natural materials she had harvested during the summer and fall. "I think it's a really lovely business because it incorporates so many aspects of what inspires me—boreal forest preservation and plant ecology, local plant use, the development of strong local communities and diversification. . . . So there are a few different ways that I get my plants—one way is I come out like this and wild harvest them myself."

Everything that Chevrette uses in her teas is either wild harvested or farmed organically. The farmed part of the equation is twofold, from an environmental perspective: it helps build value for products from the boreal forest, which in turn helps the forest be used for and seen as more than just stands of timber waiting to be chopped down. "I used two berries—I use blueberries and cranberries, and both of those I buy from First Nations who are doing non-timber forest initiatives. The blueberries I purchase from Aroland First Nation, and the cranberries from Iroquois growers from the Muskoka Region [of central Ontario]."

A FERTILE WALK IN THE WOODS

Hang out with Chevrette in a wild environment, and she'll start introducing you to her friends. "This is yarrow," she says, pointing to a cluster of tiny flowers. "This one I use in a blend called Canadian Shield—I blend it with peppermint and rose hips. This is an incredible plant. It has anti-inflammatory properties. It is an immune stimulant, and it is also a styptic, so it staunches bleeding. If you're ever out and you get a bee sting or a cut, you can make a spit-poultice. You just take some flowers, chew them up and spit them out, and put them on the burn or cut or bee sting, and it'll immediately take the sting out."

Red clover is known to even hopeless urbanites, but it has uses that we wouldn't guess when we glance at it by the side of the highway. "I use red clover in my boreal berry blend," says Chevrette. "This is an amazing plant, because it improves the function of your organs, slowly, and it helps to cleanse the blood. It's considered a master blood cleanser. It's reputed as having strong antitumor activity."

Chevrette takes us over to a beautiful cluster of berries and guides us through them, starting with a raspberry the likes of which we've never seen. "This is a dwarf wild raspberry," she says. "Raspberry is a great uterine tonic. I used it through both my pregnancies, and my pregnancies and labors were great. My first one was three hours, start to finish. They were both home water births. My second one was an hour and a half."

"This is saskatoon berry," she says, touching a larger, darker fruit. "I'm developing a new tea that uses this and a wetland plant.

"The blueberries I use in many of my blends, and they're the most antioxidant fruit of all. Of course in the north we have a difficult time growing fruit varieties, so this is our fruit."

Chevrette gestures at the little berry grove and flower patch that we've explored over the course of an hour. "Within this little spot there's probably eight to ten medicinal plants. It's typical [for the boreal forest]," she says. As she tours her woodland empire, Chevrette seems as content as a bee in patch of flowers. "How could it get any better?" asks Chevrette. "I'm out doing what I love, and I'm incorporating so many of my different passions. And I'm also bringing people a product that is healthy, that is good for the environment, it helps build community, and it creates jobs for people in terms of harvesting berries."

Boreal Forest Teas are available online at www.borealforestteas.ca.

BARRY'S BEES

BEARS' BEES AND HONEY, THUNDER BAY

"My name's Barry, and my nickname all through school was the Big Bear. When we were thinking for a name for the company, my wife said, 'Why not Bear's? Bears and honey.'" Thus was named Bears' Bees and Honey, one of the leading producers of honey in the Thunder Bay area, a rare haven for bees against the danger of colony collapse. Beekeeper Barry Tabor has been at it since the mid-1990s but has been fascinated by bees since childhood. His hobby has become a business, producing around a thousand kilograms of honey a year from around thirty-five colonies.

Although Tabor is based in Thunder Bay, he has a building 340 kilometers north of the city where he can bring bees to feast upon blueberries, Labrador tea, and firewood in order to make honeys that resemble cheap, imported, grocery store honey in the same way good Cognac resembles bottom-shelf whiskey.

Tabor's start with bees came at a young age, at his grandparents' camp near Thunder Bay. "I was five or six years old, and this bumblebee flew into the camp," he recalls. "And kids, being kids, were 'Aaaaah! the bee's going to sting!' but this gentleman by the name of Rick Angle, who was a friend of my parents, he says, 'Bumblebees won't never harm you. They'll never sting you unless you squish them.'

"So he walks over to the window where it was buzzing, and clasps it in his hands, and he held it, and he showed all of us kids. And I was absolutely from that day totally in love with bumblebees." And later in life it was through Tabor's then-beekeeping mentor that he met the woman who would become his wife. "It was a picture that was always looking at me," says Tabor. "It was a black-and-white picture, and I asked, 'Jerry, who is that?' 'Oh, that's my niece, and she's your age, and she's single!' And we ended up getting married three years later."

And so Tabor's relationship with his bees is not something simple to put into words. But the care with which he handles them and their honey is more akin to how a shepherd tends to a flock than anything else. You get the distinct sense that not only is the relationship important to Tabor, it's something complicated and ongoing, a negotiation that reads more like a conversation—"You make the honey, and I'll take care of the rest"—stated and restated from hive to hive and season to season. If you taste that in the honey, it could be your imagination, but more likely than not

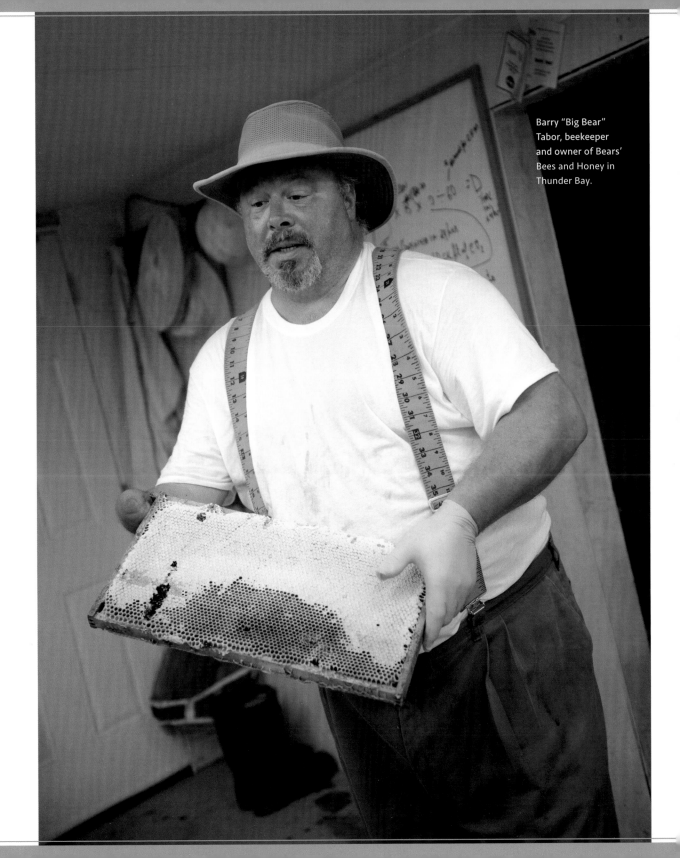

Barry "Big Bear" Tabor, beekeeper and owner of Bears' Bees and Honey in Thunder Bay.

it's something real and beautiful, difficult to write or speak but easy to sense when the sweet taste of the bee's labor hits your palate.

In terms of geography, Tabor's operation is uniquely well positioned. The Thunder Bay region of Lake Superior is a beautiful place to raise bees because, as Tabor tells it, "we're one of the only places in the world that's free of varroa and tracheal mites."

Tabor attributes this to a local beekeeping culture that doesn't import bees. "We export bees—actually, we've been exporting to Minnesota. And they're buying our bees, because they're clean."

Tabor grows his colonies and queens slowly and believes that a general lack of stress helps keep his bees happy and healthy. And that, in turn, helps them turn out some interesting honeys, including a buckwheat honey that tastes like dark caramel and wheat—almost like rye bread with honey—and the almost herbal Labrador tea honey that is a specialty of his operation. We taste his honeys out of old-fashioned glass jars in the rustic outbuilding where he separates honey from the comb. The overall effect is magic. Each variety of honey tastes distinct from one

Removing the caps from honeycomb at Bears' Bees.

A variety of honey on display at Bears' Bees.

another, and none has the depressing flatness of supermarket honey. Instead, they are vibrant with the taste of the wildflowers.

To Tabor, though, the taste of the honey is only part of the importance of what he does. The other part is the way his product helps fill a hole in the local ecosystem of food.

"I think a lot of it has to do with food security," says Tabor. "With community sustainable agriculture, one of these days we're going to end up with a situation where we won't be able to get fresh foods—well, how fresh are they?—from California, Mexico, South America, Hawaii, China, whatever . . . anyways, if you can just buy local, you're supporting your growers and producers locally."

Honey from Bears' Bees and Honey is available at the Thunder Bay Country Market. www.bearsbeesandhoney.com

BELLUZ FARMS AND THE RISE OF ACCESSIBLE AGRICULTURE

BELLUZ FARMS, THUNDER BAY

The romantic story of working the land is widely acknowledged to be just that—a story. The grit and patience required to be a farmer in a temperate climate are enough to instill respect. In the sometimes brutally cold, always challenging world of northwestern Ontario, thoughtful observers should be moved to awe.

Jodi and Kevin Belluz of Belluz Farms have been working the land since childhood. Kevin's grandparents started by growing potatoes in response to a request from the general store and moved on to the pick-your-own craze in 1972 by planting an acre of strawberries. "It just blossomed into a market garden enterprise," says Jodi. "We still grow potatoes but in a different way for a different market. We direct market 95 percent of our produce. We do a bit of wholesale with small grocery stores and restaurants, but it's mostly direct sales."

Jodi and Kevin Belluz of Belluz Farms in Thunder Bay.

The Belluz family farm is three hundred acres, eighty of which haven't been cleared and another thirty to forty of which are "marginal," as Jodi says, providing just forage and hay. The farm's bread-and-butter crop is strawberries, which take up sixty acres of the farm's land (a rotation means that only eight to ten of those acres have strawberries on them at any point in time).

It's easy to think of a farm as just a place. But if you spend a bit of time watching the anthill of activity that consumes Belluz Farms, you begin to appreciate that it's really a system. It's the weather and the soil (talk to any farmer for any length of time, and you appreciate that farming the dirt is the hard part; the crops all rise out of that baseline struggle), it's the generation of family members, it's the visitors and the food, and it's the long-term commitment required to carve sustaining order out of the chaos of nature. A farm isn't just land, it's a living organism.

The farm runs a "harvest café" during strawberry, raspberry, and pumpkin seasons. "We have ice cream, strawberry shortcake, strawberry lemonade, strawberry tarts," says Jodi. "We do corn roasts on the weekends . . . in the fall, it's all about harvest soups and pumpkin pie and apple pie. And we often have a barbecue running. We only do local meat on the barbecue—local hamburgers, local sausages."

The farm also has a shop, where we bought a bag of Red Fife flour, made from a Canadian heritage wheat. Upon our return to Minneapolis, we used the flour to bake a hearty, sesame-tasting bread. "They think it was the first kind of commercial wheat really grown successfully in Canada," says Jodi. "But as wheat got more homogenous, it became in danger of fading away. Slow Food was one of the groups that really took this on, the growing and milling it and using it again—we've been growing. It's a whole wheat flour with almost a sort of nuttiness to it."

Jodi came to the farm through working on a competitor's farm. "It's a sad, pathetic, storybook story," she says, laughing. "I worked on a competitor's berry farm, and I was best friends with their daughter, and that's how I met Kevin here on this berry farm—we were like fifteen." Jodi sees the Thunder Bay agricultural scene as blossoming. "We're a very isolated community, and we tend to be on the later end of trends," she says. "When I first came into the farm ten years ago, the big push was taste and freshness . . . a day of entertainment, a day in the country had to be wrapped up into all of that, to get people to drive out here. It's only fifteen minutes from town."

Although the Belluz farm is in a valley (and therefore receives less lake-effect precipitation than other land closer to Superior), Jodi says that the connection to the lake is palpable. "You grow up, and you feel this connection to the lake," she says. "You always know it's there. It's visually always there. You either take it for granted, and you know that there's this abundance of water, and abundance of moderate weather, and things that go along with that . . . and there's a negligence that can come along with that."

But that awareness can cut another way, she says. "Then there's those of us—particularly those of us who farm—who realize that living in the Lake Superior watershed is so integral to survival . . . to growing, and to living, from the fishing community to what we depend on for irrigation and water supply. We've got both of that going on in Thunder Bay, really. Everyone who comes from Thunder Bay has this pride and identity that you come from the lake, and that you have access to the lake."

Awareness of the importance of local food has risen, and with it, interest in making local food a serious part of the week's diet for people in Thunder Bay. "People are more aware of wanting to buy food close to home, and food security," says Jodi. "That's made our lives a lot easier—people are searching for us."

A GROWING MOVEMENT TO EAT LOCALLY

But being sought out by forward thinkers won't be enough, Jodi argues, to make community agriculture prosper in Thunder Bay. "If we want to push agriculture to the forefront and have a truly secure food supply, I think we have to start getting local food into the mainstream of Thunder Bay, and I think that has to be through institutions, like hospitals and schools, retirement homes," she says.

"And beyond that, into the grocery stores, which we can't get into at all—they all have central distribution that is far away from us. Lots of red tape. Small independently owned ones, you can, but they're not buying much. I think that's the future, not more stalls at the farmers market."

Provincial government hasn't (of yet) been of much help, Jodi says. The push for "Ontario-grown" produce tends to mean, in practice, food grown in the southern part of the province. Community organizing, however, is gaining strength.

"We have a Slow Food chapter, and we have the Food Action Network, and they

Signage at Belluz Farms displays sage food advice.

actually run through our Thunder Bay District health unit, so that's a government-run agency," she says. "And through the university we have the Food Security Research Network . . . and there's Thunder Bay Beekeepers, and a few other groups. . . . What's great about them is they're so consumer focused. And just overall media attention.

National media attention, North American media attention. . . . Most people here who care about food know who Michael Pollan is."

Restaurants have been slow to adapt, but Jodi sees rays of light. "There have been a few little independent restaurants in Thunder Bay who are starting to want to have alternatives to Sysco food delivery," she says. "And we're starting to see more fish. We used to have people come and visit us and say, 'Why can't we buy any local fish in the restaurants here? It's funny! It's strange!' We'd be like . . . 'Right, actually!' That's changing. The reflection of our seasonality, which is different, being northern of other places."

Of the Angry Trout in Grand Marais, Jodi says, "They're great! They use more of our produce than anyone in Thunder Bay. George and Barbara put thought behind everything in that restaurant—they talk a lot about 'Capitalism with a Conscience.' It's OK to make money, but can we do it in ethical ways?"

Belluz Farms, 752 Candy Mountain Drive, Thunder Bay, 807-475-5181. www.belluzfarms.on.ca

FORT WILLIAM'S EDIBLE HISTORY LESSON
AUDREY DEROY AND OJIBWA FOOD TRADITIONS

Audrey DeRoy straddles two worlds through her work as a historical interpreter at the Fort William Historical Park. As Niizho Miigwanag ("Two Feathers"), she is a native heritage specialist bringing the sights and sounds of history to visitors from the present era, and she is an ambassador from the world of the Ojibwa (or Anishinaabe) to largely European-descended guests of the fort.

Built on the site of the North West Company fur-trading fort, which was the scene of an attack by mercenaries hired by the Hudson's Bay Company in 1816, the Fort William complex includes forty-two reconstructed period buildings. "We're ensconced within a natural environment—there's far less encroachment of modern life," says Marty Mascarin, the communication officer at Fort William. "It helps to re-create this period atmosphere and take you back." The complex stands as a remarkable place of learning and entertainment, a historic tourist attraction that is one of the biggest draws to the Thunder Bay area. Costumed reenactors, playing the roles of nineteenth-

Audrey DeRoy, a historical interpreter at Fort William Historical Park in Thunder Bay, discusses Ojibwa food traditions inside a reconstructed wigwam.

century tradesmen, voyageurs, and Ojibwa, mill among the visitors and bring a sense of living history to the fort.

Under the shelter of a reconstructed wigwam, we spoke with DeRoy about historic and contemporary First Nations food practices. "We know for a fact that traditional foods have a lot of really good medicinal properties that have helped us sustain a good diet and way of life, prior to the things being put into us today," she says. Much of her knowledge of Ojibwa food is presented through the lens of native health and nature lore, a complicated system of "medicines" not dissimilar to the "humors" of the European Middle Ages or the concept of chi in Eastern healing.

"You know about the epidemic of diabetes—that's huge among our people," she says. "We love the sweetness from the maple sugar, and we ate that for generations—that was a huge food source. And now today they're finding out that maple syrup is the preferred sugar for a diabetic—and when you think about that, that's a sure sign that our diet was better for us. I find a lot of our people are going back to that. That's the transition from being reliant on grocery stores and urban life."

The challenge of sticking to a traditional diet—which can be difficult to follow even under the best of circumstances—is intensified by the ready availability of modern fast food, rich in sugar and fat. "If you don't introduce it to your children when they're babies, they'll basically turn their nose up at it, because they're so addicted to chicken fingers and French fries," she says. "Instead of frying our foods, we used to bake our foods, and we're getting back to that, too. Frying foods is terrible for our people . . . it's terrible for everybody!"

Among First Nations communities such as the Ojibwa, there is an increasing emphasis on moving away from white flours to white rice and corn flours. But not all of the old ways will be easy to return to. "I don't know if you've seen a moose around lately," she says. "I remember as a young woman we were raised on moose in the fall time, and deer meat in the late fall and winter. And then rabbits . . . still fishing, we still had fish. When spring came, there was lots of fish."

As we talk with DeRoy about Ojibwa food, it soon becomes clear that her food knowledge alone would be enough to launch a restaurant as chic and hyperlocal as the foraged food–driven Noma in Denmark, named best in the world by *Restaurant Magazine* from 2010 to 2012.

From smoked blueberries to cattail roots to wild carrots to fruit leather made of birch bark and all manner of exotic game meats, the food folkways she shares seem at once ancient and fully modern, plugged in to the seasons and the environment in the effortless manner that can come only from generations of practice. Imagine a meal of beaver tail and bear meat, served with evergreen teas and wild rice—it sounds dodgy at first but delectable when filtered through knowledge situated in the land and its flora and fauna.

"The fur traders here at Fort William were sustained on fish," chimes in Mascarin.

"But oh my goodness, have you ever tried beaver, Marty?" asks DeRoy. "We wouldn't normally get a beaver until wintertime when the coat is nice and thick—and the meat, oh the fat from a beaver in wintertime, it is so delicious. It's like eating a beef roast."

As is true with most everything wild and gamey, preparation is everything. "You just need to know how to doctor that beaver up," she says. "You put the medicines in there, and you know, those medicines will take the gaminess out of the meat. This plant is amazing, it acts like a bay leaf, it gives it flavor. I always say, cook it for a long time over low heat. Beaver, you can eat the tail, too. You just take a Y-shaped branch, and you stick it into the tail, and you roast it by the fire. And when you're done with it, you take a bite, and it tastes really greasy, but it's also crunchy, and it tastes really good."

DeRoy also sang the praises of bear and, first and foremost, its fat—a vital resource for Ojibwa surviving the lake's long, cold winters. "Have you ever had bear meat? It tastes like pork. I don't eat it, it's one of my helpers [sometimes known as "spirit animals"], but it tastes like pork. One good bear in the fall is like fifty pounds of fat. And when you think about that, we always mix fat in with our dried food, like pemmican and that, we mix dried fish with berries."

Moose, too, was once a staple food of the local peoples of the lake. We'd heard from numerous people that moose is pretty close to inedible, but DeRoy had knowledge to share: "I know people say [about moose], oh, it tastes so lousy, and I'm thinking: 'How do they cook their food?' I know watching my mom and my aunties and my uncles—the best thing with moose is first you have to hang and drain the blood out of it. If you don't do that, the moose meat will taste funny. The next thing is when you've harvested the moose, it tastes very good in the fall time because they have all the nutritious things they've been eating in the summertime. And the thing with moose meat—you have to simmer it.

"You cook it in a little bit of its juices, and a little bit of water, and you can add a bay leaf, you can use maple sugar to sweeten it a little bit, you could use wild ginger . . . all kinds of things. You start adding things to it—onions, and carrots, and celery, and things we get in the grocery stores.

"Have you ever had moose tongue? Moose nose? Oh my goodness. The nose you have to burn all the hair off, then you just roast it. It's really, really good. The tongue . . . have you ever had liver pâté? It tastes like that! It looks kind of weird sitting in the fridge, all cooked up. But it's really good." She attests to the meat's nutritional value as well: "People used to say moose meat has no nutritional value, but I was raised on this meat, how did I get so healthy? That's not true! When you look at all the good medicine those animals are eating, you're eating that medicine, too."

Beverages weren't neglected in Ojibwa cuisine, either. "All the berries are turned into drinks," she says. "We don't even drink water—it's usually mixed with maple syrup and berry juice. It's really, really good. Most of our drinks are teas. A long time ago, our people would have tea parties." "Tea" in this case means a local tisane (or herbal tea) from a plant in the heath family. "The Europeans call it Labrador tea, and it grows in swampy areas around here—our people call it muskeg or swamp tea," says DeRoy. "It's really good for you. It gives you a lot of energy, and it gives you a good feeling inside if you have a cup or two a day. You don't want to have any more than that."

You can also make teas from the green ("not rusted") leaves of strawberry plants, DeRoy says. "You dry them, and then you boil your water and put the dried leaves in. You have to use a certain amount, you can't put in a whole pile or it becomes very, very strong. You could have a strawberry drink with the strawberries watered down and a little maple syrup in there."

As DeRoy tells it, food is more than fuel—it's the web that holds a community together. Key to that relationship are local fish. "We love our pickerel," she says. "We love our sturgeon. And some people prefer to have northern pike. Suckers, white suckers, are really good smoked. A lot of our people really love white sucker when it's smoked. I love frying mine with ground-up cornflakes—oh my goodness, pickerel is one of my favorites."

But the true key to enjoying fish, says DeRoy, is sharing it with the community. "Some people purchase it because they don't have any means to go out on the water," she says. "Some people fish and gill net. That's how I get my pickerel, I go out gill netting with my partner. We don't keep it for ourselves, too, that's called a stingy box, you know, the freezer.

"You want to hand out the food. When we get a net full of fish, we share it. We share it with all the elders that we know who can't get that kind of food, the traditional food."

THE DEADLY DUALITY OF PLANTS

"What kind of vegetables would the Ojibwa be cultivating?" asked Mascarin. "Wild carrots," replies DeRoy, as she begins reciting a list of edible plants. "When I think of wild ginger, I remember my mom uprooting wild lily roots . . . the fiddlehead, we do cow parsnip, horseradish, there's those roots, too . . . Cattail roots, oh my goodness. When you boil them, there's a starch that you can use as a thickener for your stews and that, or you can dry them and make a flour out of them. So we would use those, too."

The brown tops of cattails, even before they get fluffy, can be taken for food, too. "It looks like corn, but it tastes like cucumber crossed with watermelon, and that's really good for you too. And when it does get the fluff, you can use the fluff for a thickener in your stew. Same with the wild ginger, the tops of wild ginger. I always tell people though that if you're harvesting, you have to know what you're doing. There's a duality in the plants—one is really edible, and the other is highly poisonous."

Ojibwa bread is made from cattail roots, from the inner bark of aspen trees, from corn traded from other nations, and from ground-up wild rice. Of the latter, DeRoy says, "It's kind of like a tortilla—it's really delicious, but it's heavy, eh? And nutritious. Wild rice has a lot of what cereals have in them—niacin, iron, thiamine."

As America has become one of the world's most overweight nations, the curse of fried food has fallen particularly hard on Native Americans and First Nations Canadians. Frying has no deep historical roots with the tribes, DeRoy says. Trade items like iron fry pans had a profound effect. "We never fried our bread, we baked it on a poplar stick, which allows the bread to keep its original taste," she says. "Or we would have a nice flat rock that we'd heat up and put the dough on it, and we'd keep heating the rock. You'd have a variety of rocks, before even contact, we'd have cooking rocks, just for cooking. Imagine all the experiential knowledge you'd have to obtain, by figuring out what kind of rocks are good for boiling, that wouldn't explode in your face. I've

Audrey DeRoy pops wild rice using a traditional Ojibwa method.

been in a sweat lodge where the hot water would hit rocks and they'd explode, and just be ricocheting around."

"We're going back slowly, but it's happening," she says. "The elders—parents taking charge and changing diets. And all the shows on APT Healthy Living."

Just before we leave Fort William, DeRoy does something that strikes us as a little miraculous. She prepares wild rice in a way that we've never had it before, toasted in a cast-iron pan over an open fire. It's a bit like popcorn, but smoky, woodsy, and crackling with texture. As we down handfuls of the stuff, she tells us a bit more about how it can be used.

The harvesting, husking, and drying of wild rice are among the oldest food traditions on the shores of Lake Superior and central to Ojibwa life and lore as a life- and culture-sustaining harvest ritual. "As part of removing the husks, someone would quote unquote dance on the husks, while wearing moccasins," says Mascarin. The rice, along with other foodstuffs, played a key role in the fort's survival and prosperity. "Items such as berries and maple sugar were used as trade items—it wasn't just furs," he notes.

"You know what this is good with?" says DeRoy, of the rice. "Partridge. I love partridge. I'll dig a hole in the coals, and I'll put the partridge in there, and it'll cook. I'll take it out . . . and in today's world, you have mushroom soup. So I'll dice up the partridge and put it into the mushroom soup, and pop some wild rice and sprinkle it on top. It's like getting morels and toasting them until they're crisp—the texture is the same."

An ambitious restaurateur—and "ambitious" here is shorthand for audacious, for artful, and for incredibly well funded—would partner up with DeRoy and start a restaurant to harness her knowledge, a kind of Lake Superior–driven, forage-to-table Ojibwa eatery that would host visitors from around the world and blow their minds with local food the likes of which cannot be tasted anywhere else. Hearing DeRoy share traditions relating to herbal drinks, and smoked fruit, and inspired preparations of wild game and foraged plants, the modern gourmet boggles at all the knowledge that once circulated around these shores about foods that have been so thoroughly displaced by hamburgers, pizza, and other common dishes that, quite frankly, can be had just about anywhere else.

Fort William Historical Park, 1350 King Road, Thunder Bay, 807-473-2344. www.fwhp.ca

THE CHEESE OF THUNDER BAY

THUNDER OAK CHEESE FARM, THUNDER BAY

Walter Schep, for all intents and purposes, is *the* cheesemaker of Thunder Bay. His family's company, the Thunder Oak Cheese Farm, is the only one in the area to have navigated Canada's challenging thicket of rules and regulations in order to make cheese, focusing on creamy, Dutch-inspired Gouda and Swiss. As such, it's a local touchstone. Restaurants serve its cheese on salads and burgers, and the name of the place is a point of pride. Look carefully at the menu of any of Thunder Bay's better restaurants, and there's a better than even chance "Thunder Oak" will jump out at you from the text.

Schep and his parents came to Thunder Bay from Holland, spurred by a 1968 trip his father took as an exchange student that kindled his love for the Thunder Bay area. "He was engaged to my mom at the time, and he brought her down here but made the mistake of taking the train all the way from Montreal to Thunder Bay," says Schep. "It took three days back then. Holland's not very big—you can get from one end to the other in three hours—and my mom said, 'There's no way you're going to get me to move somewhere where it takes three days and you're still in the same province.'"

But Schep's dad prevailed, and in the 1990s, the family's Thunder Bay dairy farm acquired a little cheesemaking set. "At the same time, me and my brother went to agriculture school and came back on the farm, and we thought . . . what do we do?" recalls Schep. "So cheesemaking was going pretty well, and [the cheese] tasted good, so we thought, 'Why don't we do that?'

"Both my mom's and dad's sides of the family made cheese in Holland. My mom's side of the family still makes cheese on the family farm," says Schep. "I'm a fifth-generation cheesemaker. My mom said, 'We're never making cheese,' but we ended up eating her words." In 1995, after three years of fighting through red tape, the company opened up to sell cheese to the public. "It's very expensive to get into," Schep says of the cheese business in Ontario. "It's a lot of extra work, and in Canada up here with the milk quota, you can make a pretty decent living just milking cows. There's not a real incentive to diversify."

The business milks about 75 cows out of a herd of around 180, all Holsteins, and uses only its own milk to make its cheese. Schep makes a steady 150 kilograms of

Walter Schep, cheesemaker at Thunder Oak Cheese Farm in Thunder Bay.

Cheesemaker Walter Schep forms a round of Gouda at Thunder Oak Cheese Farm.

cheese a day, Monday through Friday, working in a stainless steel, tile, and glass chamber that is three parts production facility and one part fish tank for the tourists who crowd the factory store and get an eyeful of the process.

It all comes down to row upon row of golden-hued Gouda aging out on wooden boards, geometrically perfect and the embodiment of milk's noblest destiny: to become cheese, durable and beautiful, a tribute to the land, the animal, and the man or woman who created it. To make cheese is to temper something fussy and fragile into something a bit awe inspiring, and the more you know about how it's done, the less plausible it seems. It's more magical still when you consider that Thunder Oak's cheese is the product of a reluctant family tradition, transported a thousand miles from Europe and adapted to the Canadian land and climate.

Thunder Oak won the Canadian Cheese Grand Prix in 2002 and has had cheeses place in the top ten at the World Cheese Championship in Madison, Wisconsin. The shop's flavors come in a veritable rainbow: "We do twelve different flavors," says Schep. "Everything from Jalapeno (our biggest seller) to dill to sun-dried tomato to cumin . . . we've tried a pepper cheese . . . a cardamom . . . and cranberry around Christmastime . . . I tried strawberry and it didn't work."

Seasonality is key to the cheese, says Schep—that's often the case in smaller, farmstead operations like Thunder Oak. "Our cheese is never the same. Say in springtime, the cows go outside and eat grass—the cheese will turn yellow and have a little bit different flavor," he says. "Your fats and proteins are always going up and down. . . . The biggest difference between the imported cheeses and ours is that the imports are very salty. I try to limit how much salt I add."

Schep says that an interest in local food in general (and the so-called hundred-mile diet, which emphasizes food consumed from within a hundred miles of home) has boomed in the past five years, leading to a spike in demand for his family's cheese. "I can't make enough cheese, and I wind up saying 'no' all the time," he says. "I have a distributor in Toronto who gets whatever I can't sell here, and in the wintertime I can keep him pretty happy, but when the tourist season starts, he doesn't get very much at all."

Thunder Oak Cheese Farm, 755 Boundary Drive, Thunder Bay, 807-628-0175. www.cheesefarm.ca

THE NORTH WOODS SHARK SANDWICH

KINNIWABI PINES RESTAURANT, WAWA

The Kinniwabi Pines Restaurant, near Wawa, Ontario, hits the weary road tripper like a mirage. By the time you arrive at the restaurant driving from the west, you've passed miles of empty spaces, quiet places, fallen trees, beaver dams, and, if the season is right, sprays of purple and yellow wildflowers interspersed among the massive bare boulders that line the lake's edge. On either side of the highway are massive, rough-hewn tables and walls of glacial stone, upon which you can regularly spy inuksuk, the human-like figures built of stacked rocks that once served the Inuit peoples as direction markers.

What you won't find by the side of the highway, generally speaking, is local food, or much of any food beyond the plastic-packaged, multinational fare found at gas

HOMEMADE PUMPKIN PIE AT SERENDIPITY GARDENS CAFÉ

222 Main Street, Rossport

During Canadian Thanksgiving, which falls in early October, we happened to be swinging through Rossport, Ontario, a charming little speck of a coastal town more than two hours east of Thunder Bay on the Trans-Canada Highway. As a result, we were treated to a slice of one of the best pumpkin pies we've encountered—no small praise when you consider that the entire Lake Superior region is pie country. The pie had a giant kick of real pumpkin flavor and funk, a cinnamon sugar accent, and it was served with real whipped cream—nothing fancy or unconventional but a lovely execution of an autumn classic. Visitors hoping to "get away from it all" could hardly do better than Rossport, which boasts a well-regarded bed and breakfast (The Willows Inn) and is accessible to both Sleeping Giant and Slate Islands Provincial Parks.

stations everywhere. If you spot a Tim Hortons, consider yourself lucky and pull over. Family-owned restaurants that cook from scratch are difficult to find, and outside of a little spot in Rossport, the Pines is one of the few you'll stumble across before you reach Sault Ste. Marie, Michigan, a good nine hours from Thunder Bay.

Located in the middle of a barren section of the Trans-Canada Highway where even gasoline can be difficult to come by, the Pines is an independently owned restaurant that prides itself on its food. Moreover, the food that it serves hails from the Caribbean, as distant physically and emotionally from Lake Superior's northern shore as anywhere in the world. "We came to Wawa about twenty-three years ago," says Suyin Maze, the restaurant's front-of-house manager. "Originally we bought the motel. We sold that out, but in the interim, my parents bought a restaurant and said, 'Hey, we're now in the restaurant business!'"

Although Maze's family founded the restaurant, Chef Sean Ayoung creates the food, which includes a number of island mainstays such as doubles (Indian-style flatbread sandwiching spiced chickpeas) and a sandwich including, improbably, shark meat. "When we had friends over, they couldn't believe all the flavor—the herbs and spices and fresh fish," recalls

Suyin Maze, owner of
Kinniwabi Pines Restaurant
outside Wawa, Ontario.

Maze. "Maybe because it's Third World, everything's fresh, and everyone knows how to cook—it's not fast food.

"It hasn't changed very much. Things like the liver and onions we've added in . . . the peaches and strawberries, these things we know people know. Sean studied with an Austrian couple, so he knows these European dishes [like the menu's Wiener schnitzel, pierogies, and rouladen]."

The menu's diversity, which covers Indian, Caribbean, Chinese, and local food, is part of its charm, but it's the island food that really defines its soul. "Growing up in Trinidad, we didn't have hamburgers or hot dogs. The stands, they sell doubles and shark, and other things," recalls Maze. "I try to take the kids down [to Trinidad] so they can see their family and what it's like down there, and their cousins from the States will come down. We're a Trinidadian family, so we're spread out all over. The kids get to know each other, and they stay in touch on Facebook."

The restaurant's doubles are a treat known to anyone who loves the food of Trinidad and Tobago. "It's basically [Doubles bread]—we call it back at home," says Maze. "We make it as you order it, we don't make it ahead of time." The doubles taste fabulous after a long day on the road—the crispy, warm bread perfectly cradles its spiced but mellow and soothing chickpea interior.

A DIFFERENT KIND OF HEAT

"Being Trinidadian, we don't cook with the hot peppers in the food, we add them as a condiment," says Maze. "And people find curries hot, if they're accustomed to Thai. But ours, it's . . . it's tasty. It's not burning you. It's always just added. It's not sticking in their mouths and burning them."

One of restaurant's hallmarks is the aforementioned shark, a Caribbean specialty without much precedent anywhere between Ontario and Florida. It comes from Venezuela by way of Sysco. "At home we use saltwater fish because that's what's natural—here we use what's available," says Maze. "The spices and stuff we still go down to Toronto to get—the Chinese or the East Indian spices. . . . Everything else [including shark] we get through Sysco—they come up every week with fresh produce. The beef we get from a guy we know here. Vegetables and stuff we can't count on getting, the amount—so we have to cover ourselves."

Shark sandwich at
Kinniwabi Pines Restaurant.

The restaurant has become a local mainstay, a place to celebrate special occasions and wow visitors from around the world. "We've had people from Germany and Austria and England," says Maze. I ask, tentatively, if the restaurant might also be serving a local Trinidadian community. She laughs, uproariously. "This is it for the community! You're looking at it!"

"I still love Wawa," says Maze, addressing how a family with warm, diverse global roots can find a home in such a cold and relatively empty place. "When we're away, it's great, we enjoy big-city life, but when we come back, it's nice to be home. The scenery . . . and we have four seasons. And you see the change. It never stays the same, so it's always refreshed, everything renews itself. It always makes a nice change, no matter what the season. And the peace and quiet that you have here, you can't get it anywhere else."

Once a month, the restaurant throws in another ethnic tradition, a British-style high tea. "The seniors, it's late enough in the evening where they can have something substantial. They can come out with their girlfriends and chitchat, and their

PICKLES AT YOUNG'S GENERAL STORE

111 Mission Road, Highway 101, Wawa

The charm of the old-fashioned pickle barrel is twofold: first, you're participating in a venerable frontier tradition of extracting pickles from a large communal brining barrel, and second, pickles are delicious. The pickle barrel is right in character for Young's General Store in Wawa, a combination camping/notions/souvenirs/grocery spot that is both a community center and a self-conscious warehouser and retailer of Canadian frontier nostalgia. We brought a couple of Young's General Store pickles with us while we enjoyed a shore lunch of beer-battered lake fish (the same fish we had caught while charter fishing in Thunder Bay), and their snappy bite was a perfect complement to the breaded fish's soothing kick of carbs.

granddaughters dressed up for high tea. . . . I just participate to see the kids. I love how the kids come, and they put on their finest clothes."

"On special occasions we do the barbecue out there," adds Maze. "We'll introduce wild game like elk and venison and ostrich. . . . If you overcook [ostrich], it gets harder than metal. To me, an ostrich is a feathered animal, but its meat is just like beef—it's red."

As Maze tells it, the restaurant is a special refuge in the wilderness, a place where fine food is respected by chef and patron alike. "Last year we had a lady come in from France—it was her third day in Canada," says Maze. "She had our duck, and she said— the person she was with was translating—and she was '[happy gasp] The duck is good!'

". . . Three days before she'd had duck in France at the best restaurant, and here she is dining in the middle of nowhere on the highway, and Sean makes the sauce . . . it's out of this world. 'You can't compete with the best!'"

Kinniwabi Pines Restaurant, 106 17 Highway, Wawa, 705-856-7226

OTHER EXPERIENCES ALONG THE CANADIAN SHORE

HOITO

314 Bay Street, Thunder Bay

Tastes of Finland are always close at hand in Thunder Bay, but for the most accessible and convivial, a good place to start is Hoito (which means "care"). Established in 1910 as the Finnish Labor Temple and incorporated as a communally owned restaurant eight years later, Hoito was a natural outgrowth of and gathering place for the Finnish population boom around the turn of the twentieth century. Five-dollar "comrade loans" helped the restaurant get up on its feet, and now, nearly a hundred years later, it still does a brisk business in hearty Finnish food.

Hoito was (and to some extent still is) a one-stop community center for the Finnish community, having provided shelter, union representation, theater and arts, and food to the immigrants who came here from the old country in search of jobs and new lives. This popular community pillar often has a "line-up" (as locals refer to a line) of cheerful locals waiting their turn for simple food served in a cafeteria-like ambiance.

Two treats worth trying: the kropsu (oven pancake) and viili (clabbered milk). The former is a slightly sweet, eggy treat that most readily recalls polenta, or custard, or Japanese tamago-nigiri. It's a treat when smeared with jam and eaten with a hot cup of coffee. The viili is an acquired

The Hoito restaurant in Thunder Bay is located in a building that was originally a Finnish Labor Temple.

taste, but it has an exotic charm all its own. Milk is clabbered when it's allowed to turn sour at a specific temperature and humidity, thus transforming it into an almost yogurt-like substance with a bite to it. Old treats like blood sausage and head cheese sandwiches may no longer be on the menu, but Hoito is still your best bet for a taste of Finnish working person's food on Lake Superior.

THUNDER BAY COUNTRY MARKET

425 Northern Avenue, Thunder Bay. www.thunderbaycountrymarket.com

Open year-round Saturday morning from 8:00 A.M. to 1:00 P.M. at the Canadian Lakehead Exhibition grounds on May Street, the Thunder Bay Country Market features forty to seventy vendors offerings goods including locally grown, locally milled flour (Brule Creek Farms), ginger-spiced Thai sausages by Thai-Karen's, Ukrainian food (including the almost certainly unique perogy poutine), vanilla sour cream apple pie by Jo-Mik's Baking, Chocolate Cow truffles, and more.

KANGAS SAUNA AND RESTAURANT

379 Oliver Road, Thunder Bay. www.kangassauna.ca

The establishment's slogan is "You Know You Wanna Sauna!," and we'd add, "You also want to make sure to order breakfast." The Finnish sauna tradition at Kangas is augmented by a full breakfast menu including classic, no-frills Finnish pancakes (you may know them as Swedish pancakes: extremely thin and springy in texture) served with sweet-tart lingonberry topping and real maple syrup. These plus a cup of coffee will start your Thunder Bay morning correctly, particularly in cold weather.

GILBERTSON'S PANCAKE HOUSE ON ST. JOSEPH ISLAND

3090 Huron Line, Richards Landing. www.gilbertsonsmaple.com

Ontario's largest producer of maple syrup also offers on-site dining at its pancake house near its St. Joseph Island production facility. The pancake house also has a charming gift shop containing all manner of maple syrup and maple syrup–derived products, plus the usual shirts, hats, key chains—bric-a-brac necessary to sustaining relations with nieces, nephews, grandchildren, and other gift-requiring personages. We bought a container of Gilbertson's maple syrup and found it first-rate.

THE BEER STORE

Multiple locations throughout Ontario

The Labatt and Molson Coors–owned Beer Stores enjoy a legal monopoly on beer sales in Ontario, and the result is a retail environment dominated by watery, characterless macrobrew. Some of the store's locations feature beer sold in a space that feels more like a government office than a liquor store: rows of cans and bottles behind glass on little shelves, with no evidence of local beer, seasonality, or craft-related information anywhere to be found, and clerks prohibited from recommending one brand over another. Travelers trying to solve the puzzle of why Canada's craft and microbrew options lag so far behind those south of the border should consider The Beer Store's omnipresence as a factor. Well worth visiting as a cautionary lesson in the dangers of state-sanctioned near-monopolies.

HARMONY TEA ROOM

786 I Line Road on St. Joseph Island. www.harmonytearoom.webs.com

Built in 1899 for $750, St. Joseph's Harmony Tea Room was a working schoolhouse through 1964, and its heritage shows—the interior of this charming country house is thickly clad with memorabilia from the building's school days. A photo in the tearoom shows the first full class of students (dating back to 1900); the class's teacher, J. T. Anderson, went on to be the premier of Saskatchewan.

When we visited in summer 2011, both the tearoom and the surrounding countryside were ablaze with floral color and the fruits of the field. Our cinnamon peach cobbler was a bull's-eye of flavor and texture, and everything else that we tried—finger sandwiches, an orchard salad, the tea itself—lent a pleasant, otherworldly quality to the experience, a trip through time to somewhere Victorian by way of food and drink. The tearoom is open only July through early September, so call ahead to confirm hours and state of operation.

CHARTER FISHING

It's one thing to travel around the periphery of Lake Superior, catching views of the lake through the trees and taking in the odd sunrise or sunset dockside. It's another thing to be out on the waves, casting lines into the water and catching supper. The beauty of a charter fishing trip (we went out with Archie Hoogsteen in Thunder Bay, archiescharters.com) is that your captain has you covered: a thoroughly modern boat well appointed with comfortable places to sit, three kinds of life preservers, top-notch fish-finding gear, and a half-dozen poles in good repair, dangling tempting bait into the water. The downside is that the fish don't really stand a chance—it's sport fishing but not particularly sporting. Thanks in no part to our expertise, we walked away from our charter with a lake trout and a chinook salmon, both sufficiently large to be transformed into a gourmet meal for two by the talented chefs at Lot 66 in Thunder Bay. Both fish came prepared with leeks, capers, pattypans, and a cheddar risotto. The lake trout was delicate—almost sweet and absolutely delectable. The salmon was blandly affable, taking on the character of the wine that it was cooked in. And the leftovers? A camping stove, Molson beer, and a package of Shore Lunch batter took care of them during our approach to Wawa.

SALZBURGER HOF

289 Corbeil Point Road, Batchawana Bay

The resort boasts jaw-droppingly pleasurable and relaxing views of Lake Superior's Batchawana Bay and combines the nostalgia of an old-fashioned lakeside vacation (shuffleboard, supper club dining, lawn chairs overlooking spectacular lake views) with all its downsides (swarms of screaming kids, cabins jammed together with paper-thin walls, mediocre supper club dining). Our fish fry tasted a far cry from fresh, but the German beers served with dinner were as authentic as they come, and delicious both in a general sense and in this specific, lakefront vacation context. We'd hoped to sample the lodge's famous pancakes, but breakfast doesn't start until nine, and we had to cross the border to meet interview subjects in Sault Ste. Marie, Michigan. ⬗

MICHIGAN'S UPPER PENINSULA

PASTIES, CUDIGHI, AND BIG WINES

For dramatic coastlines—the intertidal battleground where insistent waves burst against ancient rocks—you cannot beat Big Sur on the West Coast, Maine on the East, or Keweenaw on the Third.

Ted McClelland, *The Third Coast*

THERE MAY BE NO PART OF LAKE SUPERIOR with a regional identity as distinct as Michigan's Upper Peninsula. The roughly three hundred thousand UP residents, commonly and proudly known as "Yoopers," live in a world apart from the rest of their state (and certainly distinct from Wisconsin, thank you very much). Here, bracketed by Lakes Michigan and Superior, Yoopers endure frigid winters and heavy snowfalls with low-key aplomb, developing the sort of resourcefulness and coherent identity that have made proposals for splitting off into a fifty-first state (tentatively named "Superior") something more than idle chatter, if something less than truly practical.

The UP is a place where folks make their own kit wine, the Italian food is as heavy and hearty as the Cornish pasties, and snowmobiles are reliable transportation for a good part of the year. But it's also the scene of a surprising renaissance—craft brewing, local ingredients, and a vibrant dining scene in cities such as Marquette and Sault Ste. Marie, Michigan, make for a marked contrast from the Canadian side of the border (outside of the burgeoning food culture in Thunder Bay, on the other side of the lake).

Things get weird in the UP, and that's the way people like it: from the peninsula's jam-making monks, to the Gay Bar in Gay on the Keweenaw (not particularly gay but

Abandoned restaurants like this one dot the landscape of Michigan's Keweenaw Peninsula.

definitely a bar), to the often jaw-droppingly colossal industrial shipping infrastructure (both defunct and in use) in Marquette and elsewhere, there's a lot of interesting stuff to explore if you have a bit of time and an open mind.

We found some of our favorite Upper Peninsula food discoveries simply by pulling over the car and keeping our eyes open, from the forty pounds of dodgy-looking but usable apples we purchased at a gas station near Ontonagon for eight dollars (which later became several massive batches of homemade apple sauce) to the creamy, sincere, downright delicious slice of pumpkin pie purchased at the Berry Patch in the appropriately (if ambitiously) named town of Paradise.

The Upper Peninsula is connected by ferry to Isle Royale—an island that should, by all rights, probably be part of Canada's domain—and the aura of that place touches the tip of the Keweenaw Peninsula, where the boats come and go. One of the best oral histories of Lake Superior, Peter Oikarinen's *Island Folk: The People of Isle Royale*, spins some food yarns that alternate between being typical of the region and special to Isle Royale. Locals (who lacked refrigeration) would keep eggs in barrels of salt, which would help them last all season. Others ate gull eggs. Oikarinen tells the story of a family that made an angel food cake using gull eggs: "she baked it for nearly a whole day. When she took it out of the oven, it went down like a pancake." A cow—rowed from island to island to provide the animal with enough pasture to eat—also makes an appearance.

More typical to the lake as a whole is Isle Royale's aggressive do-it-yourself aesthetic, meaning struggles with home-brewed beer (which as often as not exploded), to near death by fishing misadventures, to stories of shipwrecks and cannibalism. Talk to Yoopers long enough and you'll get back to stories of a more raw, meaner time on the lake that has only recently begun to fade.

The Tower of History in Sault Ste. Marie is a great place to get a handle on this perspective, both literally and figuratively. Literally, you can ascend to the top of this 210-feet-tall Brutalist concrete tower and see both the wilderness that defines this massive peninsular society and the force of civilization as embodied by the locks and great big lake ships that pass through them. Figuratively, you can see the past and the present juxtaposed by watching the so-called educational film screened on the ground floor of the tower, which, with as much subtlety as a cannon blast, depicts savage Native Americans saved from their own cannibalistic excesses by

Ferries shuttle passengers to and from Isle Royale.

The Tower of History stands tall in Sault Ste. Marie.

saintly missionaries. The view from the tower's top is far more beautiful than that offered at its base, but both provoke thought.

The Upper Peninsula is still wild enough to evoke the destructive capabilities of the lake (through shipwreck museums and other nods to the lake's capacity as a highway for raw materials) but settled enough to have people to ponder the lake's power. Here you might well hear about the seiche (a localized storm on the lake wherein water falls then rises many feet), or the "little ice devils" of water spray that freezes on boats and eventually capsizes them in the frigid water, or the "three sisters," a brutal series of three waves that destabilize, tip, and then sink ships with no warning.

All of this, we found, was best contemplated from shore with a big mug of coffee and a thick slice of pie.

PASTIES AND PORTHOLES

KARL'S CUISINE, SAULT STE. MARIE

Karl's Cuisine is one of the only restaurants—and may in fact be the only—housed in a boat-shaped building on the shores of the lake. Its form—a geometrically cut, clapboard building with bona fide portholes rather than windows—is a salute to the maritime traffic moving through the locks of Sault Ste. Marie, just a stone's throw from this little waterside eatery with its homemade pasties and kit wine. It's also a holdover from when the building was part of the miniature golf course next door, though owner Karl Nelson was in the process of altering the boat motif with a remodel and new paint job when we visited. "I had someone comment the other day, 'You can't change the color! Everybody knows this as the gray boat!'" says Nelson. "Well, sorry, I don't like gray."

More than ten years ago, Karl and Paula Nelson started a catering business offering home delivery. The business was an outgrowth of Nelson's youth. At age fifteen, he started apprenticing at a local restaurant, with some encouragement and support from his mom ("a strong opinionated Swede"), and worked his way up: dishwasher, then prep cook, then salad guy, then saucier, and so on, all the way up. By age twenty-one, he was cheffing in downtown Detroit at the University Club. "It was an interesting job," he recalls. "We had our own parking lot there, so I felt pretty safe. You don't want to walk around downtown, especially at night."

Karl Nelson of Karl's Cuisine with his daughter, Lillian.

Karl's Cuisine in Sault Ste. Marie.

"My plan was always to start my own restaurant," he recalls. "We wanted to do fresh, local, homemade . . . which is kind of hard to find in this town. We love to go out to eat, but every place is kinda similar." Here his daughter Lillian chimes in: "Every place has their fish, their burger, maybe a steak."

"We thought, there's a real opportunity here to stand out," he adds. "All of our sandwiches are all fresh ingredients; we do artichokes, roasted red peppers, fresh mozzarella cheese . . . most of the stuff I get is through Sysco Corporation, but they use Michigan products, which we appreciate."

Karl's Cuisine has worked with farmers markets on and off but found the effort to be a struggle. "Last year, we had some problems with supply . . . and they're like double the price, and it's kind of hard for me to pass it on to my customers." Lillian adds, "And half of it, by the time it got to us, would be bad, and we'd be throwing it out."

"We're trying to work with them. I still like to go down to the market and pick things out . . . they just don't have the concept of getting a little more industrial," he says.

THE SEDUCTIVE APPEAL OF THE HUMBLE PASTY

The restaurant's locally famous pasties are made from Karl's grandmother's recipes from Iron Mountain—his grandfather was a miner. "Pasties were a big thing for the miners. They'd take them with them down into the mine shaft . . . and they'd hold it by the crust because they'd have cyanide or a poison from the mine on their hands, and then they'd throw the crust away, after having used it as a handle. She passed that on to my mother, and she passed it on to me."

"My dough is not as hearty," he adds. "We use butter, too," says Lillian.

The pasties come with homemade gravy, made from the meat, which is roasted in-house. The result is a dish that keeps locals happy while satisfying the demands of tourists, who recognize the pasty as one of the UP's signature delicacies. "A lot of the older people, they come on bus tours, and they know what they are, they know what they want: 'We want the pasties,'" says Lillian.

The restaurant's wine-making operation is a legacy of the former Superior Coast Winery, and it produces about twenty different kit wines including chardonnays, chiantis, and pinot grigios. The kits are from the Wine Expert, and the juices are imported. The standout bottle, however—at least in this tourist's eyes—is the Yooper, which comes in a duct-taped bottle and features a big, bold, fruity profile with an acidic supporting note that cuts the sugar. Fine wine, it isn't, but fun wine it certainly is.

Guests often buy wine on-site, enjoy it with dinner, cork the bottle, and take it with them for the road. "From Christmas on, I couldn't believe how much wine we were selling," says Lillian. "Our customers love that they can get a glass of wine with their meal. People love that they make it here. It's good, good wine, too, it's not like your Barefoot."

In addition to pasties, the restaurant's known for its stromboli, the hearty, Italian, spiral-wrapped, cheese-and-meat-stuffed bread that could be the pasty's long lost cousin. The Karl's Cuisine Italian stromboli features ham, salami, and basil, plus mozzarella and parmesan cheese, and a balsamic vinaigrette. "I can't believe how many strombolis I've made in a year, it's crazy," says Lillian, who sings the praises of house-made restaurant food even as she acknowledges its challenges.

Wine is a fixture at Karl's Cuisine.

"Unfortunately, a lot of places can't afford that, or they can't get good help. We have been blessed to have three great chefs, including my dad."

"We have one set of convection ovens that's always on," says Karl. "It doesn't stop. I'm kind of tight in this building, I'd like to get more space." Space is tough to come by, jammed up against the locks as the restaurant is. But like most weaknesses, the restaurant's location is also its strength. "When the ships go by, they're right there," says Karl. "You can see everything. When the wind gets blowing, water splashes out of the locks."

"One of our goals is to enclose that whole deck up there and make that the winery," says Lillian. "We'll put all the Cambros [beverage dispensers] out there with the wine."

Karl's Cuisine, 447 West Portage Avenue, Sault Ste. Marie, 906-253-1900. www.karlscuisine.com

ROOT BEER FALLS AND BLUEBERRY ALE

TAHQUAMENON FALLS BREWERY AND PUB

Michigan's Tahquamenon Falls has been a landmark for generations. It appeared on a seventeenth-century French map as "Outakouaminan" and is the setting for Longfellow's *The Song of Hiawatha*, wherein Hiawatha builds his canoe "by the rushing Tahquamenaw." These days, the tannic brown waters are often known as the Root Beer Falls.

Tahquamenon Falls State Park, which surrounds the falls, is also notable for a little two-acre blip of food-friendly real estate called the Tahquamenon Falls Brewery and Pub. Plunked down adjacent to the park's main parking lot, the brewpub serves unpretentious, eminently drinkable craft brew and locally inflected food to as many as five hundred thousand visitors, who come to the park in search of natural vistas. "It's very unique, isn't it?" notes proprietor Lark Ludlow. "I think it's the only park in Michigan—and probably in the United States—that has a brewery in it. This is on private property—it's on two private acres."

The park got its start in 1947 and now spans over 40,000 acres of woods and water. In 1949, Ludlow's grandfather was a local entrepreneur with an eye for the future. "He was one of the first people to introduce the snowmobile to the Upper Peninsula from Canada from Bombardier," recalls Ludlow. "I remember riding on it when I was six or seven, which is more than fifty years ago. I'm sixty."

"He found out about the property here and bought it from a lumber company," she says. "It was only 160 acres, which isn't much. It was the land that went right

Lark Ludlow, owner of Tahquamenon Falls Brewery and Pub.

SMOKED FISH DIP AT TAHQUAMENON FALLS BREWERY AND PUB

The brewpub at Tahquamenon Falls serves up a Lake Superior smoked fish dip that ranks among our favorites on the lake, despite (or perhaps because of) its simplicity. Speaking abstractly, if you're going to flavor a cream cheese–based dip, it helps to have a light touch. You want to taste the fish, but you don't want to be crushed by it. The brewery gets the proportions just right: the fish flavor comes through as a pleasant smoky undertone with just a hint of funk, lending depth and interest to the dip. Green onions offer freshness and texture. It's tasty stuff and a great way to start a lunch at the falls.

here to the falls. He kept 2 acres, [where] this [restaurant] is located right now, and he gave the rest to the state. And he designated where the parking lot would be, so that people had to walk and experience the forest before coming on the falls. I think that was great vision. You keep the commercialization away from the falls." The walk itself is short and gorgeous, and Ludlow's right—the stroll through the woods helps build up to the sight of the tannic water cascading down the rocks.

In 1987, the land passed to Ludlow and her youngest brother. An indoor restaurant seemed to be the answer to the proliferation of bugs and occasionally inclement weather that can make a food stand a gamble, even in summer, and a brewery seemed to be a natural fit for the location. "I said, 'You know, microbreweries are on a high climb in our country, and there aren't any in the UP,' and at the time there weren't. 'Wouldn't it be cool if you came out to the forest, and you think you're going to have this beautiful experience . . . but wouldn't it be even greater if you could top it off with a beer?'"

The beer is, like many in vacation country, balanced but light on its feet, with little of the hops or spice bombs typical to urban craft beers. "In other words, I don't make an IPA," says Ludlow. "I have only four fermenters, and I make 310 gallons at a time. It's a ten-barrel system, and I've got to be able to produce it quickly. And I've got to have it sell. And that's why it's lighter. I like to go lighter on the fruit."

FROM MACROBREW TO MICROBREW

When Ludlow started the business in 1990, she found herself educating locals and tourists alike on the restaurant's brew, coaching them to step up from watery macrobrews into the mild but more flavorful product offered at the brewpub. The restaurant's peach beer, for example, is very light and balanced, with a clean, natural taste. "I don't want it to taste like cough medicine," says Ludlow. "I just try to make it natural. I name things after the area whenever possible.

"I don't want people to get wasted here—that's not the idea. And we're not a late-night place. And people don't sit here all day at the bar. We want them to be able to drive away, we're in the middle of nowhere."

The brewery's potable signature may well be its blueberry beer. "The base is a good wheat ale," Ludlow says. "You need a real good product for the flavoring—a natural flavoring is best. I started it as . . . my contribution to the blueberry festival, which is the third weekend in August of every year. And that's how I got it going. And now

Fish and chips at Tahquamenon Falls Brewery and Pub.

everybody's doing it." Trips to the Vierling Restaurant and Marquette Harbor Brewery in Marquette, Michigan, or the Boathouse Brewpub in Ely, Minnesota, confirm this: blueberry beer has really caught on around the shores of Lake Superior.

The brewpub's food is modest but made with care. The smoked whitefish dip made from fish smoked in Paradise, Michigan, stands up among the best of those served along the shores of Lake Superior, and the pasties are made locally. "We do mostly scratch cooking," says Ludlow. "We make our own soups—this wild rice soup is good. The wild rice comes from the great state of Minnesota. We make our own beer batter. If you have the whitefish, you can have it beer battered, lightly breaded, or broiled."

Such food would be enjoyable nearly anywhere, but discovered serendipitously in the shadows of one of the Upper Peninsula's natural landmarks, it's especially savory—and an example of how fine eating and the natural world often travel shoulder-to-shoulder on the shores of Superior.

Tahquamenon Falls Brewery and Pub, Tahquamenon Falls State Park, M-123 Upper Falls Drive, Paradise, 906-492-3300. www.tahquamenonfallsbrewery.com

EATING AND DRINKING ITALIAN IN MARQUETTE

CASA CALABRIA, MARQUETTE

The first thing we asked Phil Johnson of Casa Calabria in Marquette about was his restaurant's cudighi, or Italian sausage sandwich. A cudighi is a native to the Upper Peninsula, but its twin brother is the St. Paul sandwich known (not without controversy) as the "hot dago," a combination of marinara, sausage, mozzarella, and giardiniera on toasted bread. The Casa Calabria version is delicious, and its origin is storied. "From what I understand, [one of my uncles] went to Chicago and got this recipe," recalls Johnson. "In the early sixties, my grandfather had a sandwich shop and this [cudighi] is all they sold. Except his were in link form. He'd cook them in links and slice the link in half and fold it flat on the bun.

"Now, my grandpa . . . he'd only let one person in the shop at a time. And you're getting it with mustard and onions. He had this big butcher knife there, and if somebody wanted to order it with ketchup or something, he'd slam that knife on the table! 'You have it with the mustard! And with the onions!' and he'd slam that knife on the table. So that's how people learned to eat 'em, with just mustard and onions back then."

The tradition became a part of local lore, and a fixture for kids growing up in the area. "His wife, after he died, sold them out of her house until probably about five years ago. Her house was across the street from Ishpeming High School, and the kids would go over there and buy their cudighis. That's how she got by, selling sandwiches, just like he did.

Phil Johnson *(right)*, owner of Casa Calabria in Marquette, with his staff.

The cudighi sandwich at Casa Calabria.

"We still get those customers in here who are sixty, seventy, eighty years old who order them with mustard and onions," Johnson says. Johnson's family history in the restaurant business dates back to 1953, with the opening of the first Barbiere's restaurant in Milwaukee, Wisconsin. "It was my Uncle Tony's," recalls Johnson. "In the sixties the brothers branched out and opened their own places—in Marquette, in Ishpeming, and Negaunee—that's been sold. Counting the ones that have been started by employees who have bought out my uncles, there have been twenty-three that have been opened. Ours is the thirteenth. We've been in business for thirty years as of July 1."

This staple of the Marquette dining scene is one of a number of compelling places to eat in the area. Like many town-and-gown communities, the twenty-thousand-person city of Marquette punches out of its weight class in terms of amenities and charm. Northern Michigan University (total enrollment is ten thousand) is among its biggest employers, but strong shipping and mining industries laid the foundation for its current prosperity and gave the city its strongest visual symbol, the massive, science fiction–evocative Lower Harbor Ore Dock, which juts out into the lake. Much iron ore is still shipped from Marquette, a major port on Lake Superior. If you've seen Otto Preminger's highly respected film *Anatomy of a Murder*, you know a bit about

Marquette; the film was based on the book by Ishpeming native and attorney, judge, writer, and fly-fisherman John Voelker.

Finns, Germans, and Italians make up a large percentage of the town's population and give its food much of its charm and flavor. "Typically the southern Italian food is simple and a lot of red sauces and white sauces," says Johnson. "My grandfather typically made things with meat. But you guys [DePetros] cooked all them noodles—ravioli and stuff—where we didn't in our family. Egg noodles, but not actually all the raviolis and stuff." Here Johnson gestures at Tom DePetro, a family friend who has joined the interview with several bottles of homemade wine. "Growing up, my mom would cook spaghetti, and put pork roast in it," recalls DePetro. "Basically whatever meat they had they'd throw in the spaghetti sauce—whether it'd be pork chops or spareribs or chicken or whatever—they all had a different flavor, because the meat is different."

"My grandpa made bread almost every day—it's just what you did," recalls Johnson. "My mom had thirteen kids in the family, that's how you got by. You had a big family, too. How many brothers and sisters did your dad have?"

"He had seven," says DePetro. "Seven brothers and sisters."

CRANBERRY CREAM CHEESE BREAD FROM THE NORTH STAR BRICK OVEN BAKERY

Michigan 123, Newberry.
www.exploringthenorth.com/northstar/bakery.html

Cranberry cream cheese and wild cranberries go into the sourdough cranberry cream cheese bread made in the woods near Paradise, Michigan, at the North Star Brick Oven Bakery, a middle-of-the-woods anomaly that creates gourmet breads in a brick oven in a shack in the wilderness. The bread is hearty but balanced, a treat as the base of a turkey sandwich or just happily gnawed on while walking in the woods. Owners Joanne and Paul Behm can tell you stories, such as the time Paul crossed three roadblocks to rescue their cat from the bakery during a forest fire, and the explosion of morel mushrooms the following spring.

DePetro's wine is enjoyed by Tom DePetro and Phil Johnson at Casa Calabria.

BIG FAMILIES, BIG WINE

For DePetro and many Italians in the Upper Peninsula, life and wine were (and still are) deeply intertwined. And the economical—and traditional—way to get wine was, quite simply, to make it. "When I was growing up—and it seemed like the coolest thing to me, at the time—they used to have a semi back up to the house, and they'd unload all the grapes," recalls DePetro. "And all [my dad's] buddies would be there helping to unload the grapes."

It was an annual ritual, every fall. Huge wooden crates of grapes from California would fill the DePetro basement, and the family would start the process of turning the grapes to wine. "What we've been doing now is my dad has a big arbor in his backyard, so we've been getting between three hundred and five hundred pounds of grapes," says DePetro, of his family's shift to a local product. Plums are grown and made into wine, too.

The DePetro family production is down, now, to twenty to thirty bottles from oak barrels that his father used to make. DePetro remembers a family friend who would help with the process: "To press it, he'd have us get on the press and stand on that thing, and crank on it . . . and my dad would just sit there and watch and have a sip of his wine," he recalls. "He and my dad would be sitting there drinking wine and talking, and I'd be there for hours . . ."

The common thread that comes out of talking to Johnson and DePetro is one of thrifty pleasures made luxurious through the shared experience with friends and family. What Johnson says of the meatballs could go for the full menu at Casa Calabria: "They're simple," he says. "Because of the simplicity, it's not overly spicy, and I think a lot people like that. My grandfather's theory was we had a lot of kids in our family, so we have to keep it simple."

The restaurant's garlic bread is the reliable standby for local hockey teams, who treasure the fact that it's gigantic and almost improbably buttery. We tried the stuff and loved it—it's not complicated, but it's a love letter from the world of dairy richness and garlicky pungency.

Casa Calabria, 1106 North Third Street, Marquette, 906-228-5012. www.thecasa.us

A MEAL THAT FITS IN YOUR HAND

LAWRY'S PASTY SHOP, MARQUETTE

Pete Lawry's grandparents started their eponymous pasty business in 1946, using a recipe straight from Cornwall via his grandfather's mother. That recipe—"the first fast food," as Pete Lawry tells it—was the cornerstone of the business then, as it is now. "Pasties were the thing that sold the best," he says. "You could just drive up or drive through—it had a drive-through window before McDonald's even did. You could drive up, grab a pasty and go, because they were all ready ahead of time."

The hearty pasty is a food that feels custom-made not just for mining but for cold days and nights in the Upper Peninsula. It's hearty—with a thick, crunchy, lard-based crust and a meaty, stew-like interior—and it's durable, meaning that it can serve as

Pete Lawry of Lawry's Pasty Shop in Ishpeming.

food on the go, whether that's in the mines (which still employ thousands in the Upper Peninsula), at a hunting camp, or during an office commute.

"The tradition was in the old days that they'd put the leftovers—a roast and potatoes, for example—in a pie crust," say Lawry. "You could bake it in the morning and wrap it up in newspaper or whatever, and the guys could take it to work, and it would stay hot. It'd be a hot hearty meal, and it was easy to take with you."

The continuing popularity of Lawry's pasties—and pasties in general—is a little perplexing but quite charming. They're such blunt, softly spoken, unsexy foods— lumps of lardy dough, meat, and potatoes—they don't seem to have any place in the modern food environment of wraps and sushi and bibimbap and forty-five-dollar steaks. And yet, they're a lovely and complete meal rendered in dough and meat and vegetables, an unpretentious, fully satisfying portable stew that provides nutrition and comfort at any time, and a hearty rush of real pleasure on a cold day, when the pasty seems to warm (and keep warming) you from within. Lawry's pasties can be ordered online and shipped around the country, a reflection of the nostalgia that people feel for their UP roots and the power of food to be far more than the sum of its parts.

We tried dozens of different kinds of pasties while researching this book and another (*Minnesota Lunch: From Pasties to Banh Mi*), and Lawry's are at the top of the heap in terms of traditional interpretations of the food. They aren't greasy, they don't stint on the meat, and they are profoundly satisfying, like any good, humble soul food eaten anywhere.

"We haven't changed the recipe since we started in 1946," says Lawry. "We have machines that help us peel potatoes and food processors, but we still cut our meat by hand—we grind it after we cut it—we use locally grown potatoes, we still make everything by hand . . . we make all of our crust and mix our batches by hand . . . everything is fresh, handmade, local when we can."

About that local flavor, Lawry says, "We get our meat from a distributor in Iron River . . . [the rutabagas] come from Canada, usually. We have a grower from over by Escanaba, and he delivers potatoes every week, but he runs out of stock, so most of the summer, we're scrambling for potatoes . . . so we'll have to go to Sysco, but most of the time they're Michigan potatoes."

PASTIES TO GO, AND GO, AND GO

Tourists cart away piles of frozen pasties during the peak season of the summer, and U.S. Department of Agriculture certification means that the shop can ship its product everywhere, on dry ice. "On the week of Christmas last year, we shipped 120 orders," Lawry says. "That's a big growing part of our business." During summer weeks, the shop makes about six hundred pasties, a number that declines to two or three hundred, depending, he says, on the weather.

The Lawry recipe is just beef (many others call for pork) with potatoes, onions, and rutabagas. Round or chuck steak is at the heart of the pasty, with hamburger for flavor. The shop sells traditional beef pasties and a vegetarian version ("I don't even like to call it a pasty," says Lawry, grinning), plus sandwiches. The prices are beyond reasonable: a twelve-ounce pasty was $4.19, and the seventeen ounce was $4.90, easily enough food for a couple hungry travelers.

The Lawry crust is still made, as Lawry tells it, the old-fashioned way: "Flour, shortening, water, and salt. It's very short, more short than most people make it. It's made to be durable and hold up rather than be flaky and fall apart. I think we have the corner on the crust. There again—we don't put any preservatives in our stuff. We don't put whiteners in our potatoes, we don't put any conditioners in our dough—

PASTY FROM LAWRY'S IN ISHPEMING OR MARQUETTE

A good pasty has a lot of meat, a tender interior, a tough but soft crust that contains its contents without imprisoning them, and a healthy kick of fresh potato flavor. By that reckoning, the pasty from Lawry's is as good as they come, an honest, hardworking meal fit for a (very hungry) king or a serf. Ours held up and stayed warm during a two-hour drive, so don't worry about the durability of these pasties.

just about everybody uses MSG in their potatoes—we soak them the day before to get the starch out . . . we never try to hold them longer than that."

Lawry, like his fellow Yoopers, feels good about where he is: "The community is doing fantastic," he says. "Marquette is healthy, we have a hospital, we have the mines, we have Northern Michigan University with a lot of students . . . It's a nice town, and it's growing. We're known for our cleanliness, our friendly people, beautiful weather in the summer, beautiful weather in the winter . . . if you like snow! You live here, you have to ski, or sled dog, or snowmobile, or something to get out of the house."

Lawry's Pasty Shop, 2381 U.S. Highway 41 West, Ishpeming, 906-485-5589, and 2164 U.S. Highway 41 West, Marquette, 906-226-5040. www.lawryspasties.com

BEER MEETS NATURE

KEWEENAW BREWING COMPANY, HOUGHTON

"I spent a lot of time on the other side of the bar," says Keweenaw Brewing co-owner Paul Boissevain, explaining his preparation for his current line of work. He and his partner, Richard Gray, were in the oil business in Denver for about twenty years, and it was there that they fell in love with the local brewpub. "He and his wife had gone to school up here, and they'd always wanted to retire up here," says Boissevain of Houghton. "He always said the only drawback to this place was there's no good beer. So there was an opening for us."

"[Gray] brought me up for a week, and I thought it was great," he recalls. "People kind of shake their heads. 'You came from Boulder, Colorado, to come here?' And I'd say, 'Everything I liked to do in Boulder required an hour and a half drive through traffic to get to the mountains.' Humanity was everywhere. Here, a bad day at the beach, there's somebody else there."

In 2003, Boissevain and Gray started their project, which officially commenced with the opening of their building in Houghton in 2004. A few years later, they opened a production facility farther north, and now the brewery bangs out case after case of cans of beer—about one a minute. The brewery's production is split roughly fifty-fifty between cans and kegs, canning a surprisingly high number of different varieties

Keweenaw Brewing
co-owner
Paul Boissevain.

(five, as of 2011.) The beer makes its way all over the state of Michigan and into parts of northern Wisconsin, too. The latter is a tough territory for the brewery, though: "We've won a number of best of shows in the Wausau and Stevens Point area, but we still can't sell beer there," says Boissevain. "Part of it is that the distributor doesn't get the concept, and part of it is that we're not from Wisconsin."

The cans are key to Keweenaw Brewing's philosophy. "It's an outdoor environment out here," says Boissevain. "If I want people drinking my beer, I want them enjoying it outside, that's the big draw up here. And I hate broken glass on the beach. You don't want it out fishing, you don't want it rattling around in your snowmobile, and the fraternities up here don't allow bottles in."

Canning is also good for the beer. Cans block out light, which leads beer to deteriorate and eventually go skunky, and the canning process is easier on the equipment than bottling; a crushed can is easier to extract than an exploded bottle.

PANNUKAKKU FROM SUOMI HOME BAKERY AND RESTAURANT

54 Huron Street, Houghton

Like the Hoito Restaurant in Thunder Bay, Suomi is a Finnish working person's joint—a cross between a humble American breakfast diner and a Finnish cafeteria. Try the pannukakku, which is where custard meets omelet, creamy and tender, naturally sweet with a bit of vanilla flavor and heavenly with tart lingonberries. We paid $4.15 for this treat while at Suomi; $4.50 would have gotten us a breakfast featuring two sausages, coffee, and a big Finnish pancake.

OLDE ORE DOCK SCOTCH ALE FROM KEWEENAW BREWING

Keweenaw Brewing targets its beers toward the general public, moderating its use of hops, exotic flavor additives, and mind-crushing alcohol content in favor of smoother, more approachable craft beers that are a smooth transition for the Miller Lite set. Slightly more aggressive relative to its typical brew but still mild compared to the Surlys and Dogfish Heads of the world, the brewery's Olde Ore Dock Scotch Ale references one of lake's most striking landmarks, the ore dock of Marquette, Michigan. It has the malty, bourbon-like depth of a classic Scottish Ale with a lower alcohol by volume and a cleaner finish—it's Scottish Ale light and less challenging and more sessionable as a result.

A LIGHT TOUCH

The beer is perfectly suited to its environment, neither a full-fledged, deeply flavored craft beer nor a characterless macro. The brewery's ales—blonde, amber, brown, black, and the oaky, slightly more hopped Olde Ore Dock Scotch—are all about 5 percent alcohol (light for a craft beer, strong for a macro) with fewer than twenty IBUs (a measurement of hops-imparted bitterness), meaning that they're relatively gentle on the palate.

"Our beers are made for the great outdoors, and you don't want a Bell's Two-Hearted Ale or some big heavy ale while you're sitting out on the boat in the hot sunshine," says Boissevain. "It's lighter and easier to drink. Part of the business strategy is I'd rather have college kids come in and drink four beers than one or two. And we get a lot of wine drinkers who don't like beer who will try ours and sit down and drink it."

The brewery's beers tend to lead with malt or yeast, leaving the hops behind. Their mild nature is particularly on display when people sample the dark Widow Maker. "At beer shows, people will ask what's your lightest beer and we'll pour the Widow Maker, and people will say, 'No, no, no, I don't like dark beers,' and we'll say, 'Close your eyes and drink it.' It's 98 percent positive response from people."

Boissevain is anything but pretentious when it comes to his beers. Ask him what they go with, and he'll say "hamburgers and hot dogs." And ask him about staying small and independent, and he'll say, "If Coors called me tomorrow, I'd sell. And if they don't call, I'd have a great time doing this. We're both pushing sixty—I don't want to do this when I'm eighty."

"For a lot of brewers, it's 'how big can I make this beer?'" says Boissevain. "They're nice with a cigar and things . . . but there are a lot of problems out there in the world that after one or two beers, you won't be able to get through it. It takes a six-pack."

Keweenaw Brewing Company, 408 Shelden Avenue, Houghton, 906-482-5596. www.keweenawbrewing.com

The Widow Maker is a black ale from Keweenaw Brewing.

KICKING OUT THE JAMS WITH FATHER BASIL

SOCIETY OF ST. JOHN MONASTERY AND THE JAMPOT BAKERY

The Keweenaw Peninsula is—on a lake known for its wild beauty—one of the most captivating single places on Lake Superior. Jutting miles out into the water, the peninsula is covered in trees and dotted with slowly dilapidating buildings from the area's

Father Basil stands proudly in front of jars of jam at the Jampot on the Keweenaw Peninsula.

once-booming copper mining operations. The peninsula is remote, quiet, and wild, serviced by a couple of well-maintained but largely deserted highways that stretch from the charming little town of Houghton all the way up to Copper Harbor.

Near the tip of the eastern side of the Keweenaw Peninsula, just off of Highway 26 and among woods of humbling beauty, is a mostly undeveloped, six-hundred-acre community of five monks from the Society of St. John established in 1983. "It's a good

place to be," says Father Basil, who heads up this group of monks. His eyes twinkle as he tells the somewhat improbable story of the monastery and its bakery, the Jampot.

Before coming to the spot, he recalls, "We had not in fact visited here, but we looked at a lot of topographic maps, and we liked the relationship of the land and the lake and the fact that there were not many settlements—it seemed like a good place. We were in Detroit at the time, and we told friends what we were seriously contemplating, and they were horrified—they said, 'Oh, this is sheer insanity! You guys are certifiable, there's no doubt about it. But you can cure yourself! Just go in the winter and you'll never have another thought about moving there permanently.'

"So we took their advice and came here in February, and we loved what we saw."

We asked Father Basil: In the middle of brutally cold wilderness, what exactly was there to love? "Snow," he says, with conviction. "Lots of it. And nobody. It was very quiet. We were unsure what kind of accommodations might be available out in the resort area so we stayed in Houghton. I remember leaving Houghton, it must have been on a Saturday, just as the sun was coming up, probably about eight o'clock or so. The trees were covered in hoarfrost, with the sun coming through them—it was just like something out of a fairy tale. We came through Hancock, Calumet, Mohawk, back to Mohawk . . . from Mohawk back to Mohawk we did not encounter a single oncoming vehicle and that kind of sold us."

The Society of St. John's Web site puts winter and the isolation of the monastery's location into a greater spiritual and practical perspective:

> We are building a monastery in Michigan's Keweenaw Peninsula. For this reason we came to Jacob's Falls on the shore of Lake Superior nearly twenty-five years ago, and this is why we are here today: to embrace the struggle of life in a hard place, to heed the counsels of the monastic fathers, to come to know God through personal and liturgical prayer, and to beg His mercy upon ourselves and upon the whole world.
>
> While not arid, the Keweenaw is for much of the year nearly deserted. The deep winter snows make travel chancy and difficult, and there is no industry. The beauty of the land draws many visitors during the fair days of summer and autumn, but with winter's inexorable return, they depart and quiet reigns again. The winter solitude and the healing presence of the Great Lake make this a good place to live out the monastic tradition.

SPIRITUAL AND CULINARY PIONEERS

Monks have long been the living memory of the church; therefore it's no surprise that Father Basil is a font of information about his community and the land that surrounds it. He tells stories with a wit and precision that would put most working journalists to shame. "Our first winter here, which would have been the winter of '83/'84, we were trying to decide what to do to make a living," Father Basil recalls. "Monks always support themselves by some sort of enterprise, be it farming or whatever. The only thing we could think of was to harvest the wild fruit as many people were doing and make jam. At that point, a lot of people were doing it, and we'd see people with tables by the side of the road hawking jars of jam. We thought, "'Well, it's a humble thing to do. But it makes use of the natural bounty of the area, and it gets us out into the country, and so forth.'"

So the monks foraged berries and made jam the first two years, working from the little building and rudimentary kitchen that is the heart of the Jampot. The space was once a short-order restaurant, so it seemed like a natural fit. The business proved to be a natural fit with the area, too. The first two years, with no signage or retail, "but with doors and windows wide open for ventilation to remove that steam," recalls Father Basil, the monks sold twenty cases of jam.

The monks were, in effect, jam pioneers, oper-

THIMBLEBERRY JAM AND ABBEY CAKE FROM THE JAMPOT

Although the Jampot's abbot describes thimbleberries as tasting, well, like thimbleberries, we tried to put a slightly finer point on it: they are sweet, mild, and bright, with a delicate flavor—less punchy than raspberries but with a bit of seedy texture. They make a subtle jam, perfect for appreciating on toast.

Think "gingerbread fruitcake of the gods" and you have a good sense of Abbey Cake, a bourbon-, apricot-, raisin-, and nut-laden miracle of a baked good. It's easily the best fruitcake we have ever tried. Not oversweet nor overboozy, it certainly packs a punch, and it lasts close to forever when kept wrapped in cheesecloth and plastic. This has become a holiday tradition for us—there's really nothing quite like it.

ating on the edge of civilization and—locally, at least—the bounds of human knowledge. "A lot of things we were making jam out of, [commercial gelatin maker] Sure-Gel had never heard of," he recalls. "So you'd have to say, 'Well, this is sort of like . . .' and then experiment, and then troubleshoot. Sometimes it didn't set, sometimes it set too quickly."

Pin cherries were a particular challenge, thanks to a misleading name. "We said, 'Well, it's a cherry! Let's try the recipe for a cherry.' We stirred the pectin in and immediately it began to gel. They had a lot of their own pectin, which cherries are not supposed to have. So we had to adjust the recipe."

The third season, the monks began getting help with the picking, and by the fourth year, they had outsourced the time-consuming work to locals, dedicating their time to cooking and canning. The Jampot now offers dozens of different products. Any with the word *wild* on the label, explains Father Basil, are locally harvested, but some things are bought commercially. "The orange crop, for instance, doesn't come through in most years," he says with a smile.

"We do have a few wild cranberries, but the person who used to pick those has gotten too old to go out," says Father Basil. "He was a fanatic. He believed it was best to get the cranberries as late as possible after the frost so they'd be sweeter. He would go out and there would be snow, four or five inches. He'd come with a whisk broom and brush the snow and pick the berries. That man's a rare sort."

FAITH THROUGH THE LEAN YEARS

During the early years of the operation, finances were very tight. "There was some serious speculation that we wouldn't survive the first winter," says a half-serious Father Basil. "We had no insulation in the house, and an inadequate wood supply, and no money. Never any money. I remember when we first moved into the place . . . and it was just a rundown . . . well, it was supposed to have been a resort, but I've always said that must've been a euphemism. It really was the last resort.

"We met one of the neighbors our first or second day we were here. He said, 'Well, what are you doing here?' We explained we were starting the monastery and everything. He kind of looked at us skeptically and said, 'You going to be here this winter?' We said 'Sure!'

The charming cottage exterior of the Jampot.

"He said, 'Well, I'm closing my place up, and I'll be back in the spring. I'll drop in and say hello if you're still alive. Frankly I think you've got about as much chance as a snowflake in hell.'"

With difficulty—considerable difficulty—the monks made it. "Being by the lake was always a consolation during those times," he recalls. "There were many times we had only the view, but the view somehow was enough. It was wonderful to be there in the midst of the storms. Surprisingly, although there was no insulation, the building was tight. We did a lot of the services by candlelight, and even in the strongest windstorms, the candles didn't flicker."

Unfortunately, the building didn't hold any heat. "We could make it tolerably warm by starting fires in the cookstove and the parlor stove and cranking them up full bore, but whenever the fires would die down, the heat was gone," he recalls. While the jam making is a way for the monks to stay physically active and to support their operation financially, it's also a way to talk to the public about their mission. "I talk to thousands of people over the course of a year—it's an opportunity to spread knowledge of the monastery, and to answer their questions, and in some cases to pray for them," says Father Basil. "There was a woman who came through earlier this year who was suffering from ovarian cancer, and she came and she asked for prayers."

"Monasteries are usually walled off, so to speak," he adds. "And we do attempt to maintain that separation. Nonetheless, it's good to have some contact, too. So this aspect of it definitely serves a spiritual function." The work itself is part of the monk's relationship with God and His world, he says. "Many of the tasks that the monks do in the kitchen can be quiet," he says. "Granted, there's machinery going on, mixers whirring, fans blowing, but nonetheless the mind can be free because much of the work is routine and rote. Stirring jam is not the world's most engaging occupation. You have to be attentive, you have to make sure it doesn't scorch, you have to see, particularly in the case of thimbleberry and raspberry, there might be little bugs that'll come to the surface, and you have to skim and toss that stuff out. But otherwise, you're free to contemplate."

The Jampot's Web site relates a story of "Scoofies," tiny, joyous, hardworking elves who live in the gorge of Jacob Creek on the Keweenaw Peninsula. Out of the context of their peninsular paradise, they sound charming but ridiculous, but the story snaps into focus once you're out among the woods and water, away from the bustle of modern civilization and lost to the pull of the lake and its rocky shoreline. It's not hard to see the Scoofies as living symbols of this wild place's appeal: a refuge for monks seeking simplicity and a day-to-day connection with the spiritual and physical creations of God, and a recharge for secular visitors who are able to make the trek and—perhaps just for an afternoon—stop updating Facebook long enough to truly live in the moment and wonder at the beauty of the natural world. And, of course, enjoy a thick, gorgeously powerful slice of Abbey Cake for the road.

STARTING FROM SCRATCH IN THE SCRATCH JAM BUSINESS

Father Basil came to the jam-making business with no experience, having never made the stuff before in his life. His mother had made jam while growing up on a farm near Marquette in the Upper Peninsula, and she'd vowed never to can or preserve again after leaving. "I remember growing up and saying, 'Mom, everybody else's moms are putting up beans, and tomatoes, and everything else, wouldn't you do some canning for us?' And she looked at me and said, 'We did that when we were poor. I'm not going to do that again.'

"I suspect my grandmother got a great deal of satisfaction out of it, but the kids who were just chore animals . . . probably did not appreciate that," Father Basil says. Growing up, he recalls, local men mined iron in the central part of the Upper Peninsula. "Here [on the Keweenaw] they mine copper," he says. "My brother told me that the old-timers back in Marquette County used to envy the copper miners in the Keweenaw, because they were digging through rock and so had fewer cave-ins. This is something to be envious of . . . that shows you the nature of that particular occupation."

The Jampot's signature product is thimbleberry jam, which has a bright but delicate, almost herbal flavor to it. When we ask him about it, Father Basil perks up noticeably: "Of course, thimbleberry jam, everybody wants that!" Well, we ask, what's it like? "It's like thimbleberry jam!" More helpfully, he adds, "It's like a raspberry, only different. There's a little difference in shade. The thimbleberry has smaller seeds and more of them. The berry itself looks like a flat raspberry, but it is a brighter red color. They're all over the building here."

Father Basil carefully inspects a jar of jam.

And so they were. The building was enrobed in thimbleberry bushes, which helped complete the feeling that we weren't so much in a real place as in a very old fairy tale. The stuff is delicious, and it's expensive (three half-pint jars cost $36 online, plus shipping), but there's a reason for the price: "They're time consuming," says Father Basil. "First of all, you don't pick them. If you pick them with your thumb and finger, all you're going to get is a handful of seeds and juice. You cup your hand beneath it, and you just kind of pry it off with your thumb. And when it is ready, you've got about—at best—thirty-six hours to get that berry off the cane and into your bucket."

After that short, thirty-six-hour window, the berry drops from the cane, dries up, and begins to mold, presuming it's not eaten by local wildlife. "I remember some years ago, there was a woman who used to sell us domestic raspberries, and she had a large area behind her house with thimbleberries, and she'd make jam," says Father Basil. "She'd come in one time to sell us raspberries, and I asked her one day—it was hot, a very hot day in August—I said to her, 'How are the thimbleberries?' She said, 'I've never worked so hard in all my life! I go out about noon and I pick the patch. Then I go out at six, and I pick the patch. Then I'm out there again the next day, about noon. And I don't think I'm getting them all!'

"She was pretty compulsive, but if you're going to be thorough, you need to go over your patch every day for two to three weeks. They don't ripen in one place . . . there's one here, and one here, and all the rest are green."

To Father Basil's knowledge, no one has successfully cultivated them. The extensive labor required to pick and process them aside, "They always seem to grow in the darnedest places," he says. "They grow in the rocks, and they're about chest high, so you can't see, and people will twist their ankles while going in for the berries."

While the Jampot is famous for its preserves and spreads, it offers another

Muffins and other baked goods are also for sale at the Jampot.

compelling specialty: the Abbey Cake. The monks began making cakes in the middle to late eighties to provide an easy-to-ship product that could be promoted in their newsletter. The Abbey Cake is a wonder, a reminder of why fruitcakes were once treasured and enjoyed. "It's a simple fruitcake with molasses batter, raisins, and walnuts and aged in bourbon," says Father Basil. "There were two elderly ladies looking at the fruitcakes, and I was describing the Abbey Cake and how it was preserved in bourbon, and one of them raised her eyebrows and said, 'Well . . . if you have to get old . . . what better way?'"

The dense, dark, flavorful cake comes wrapped in cheesecloth and bagged, and if kept in a pantry, it can stay moist and delicious for an entire holiday season, to be sliced and shared with tea or coffee, surprising and pleasing its tasters with a smorgasbord of nuts and fruits.

Beyond jams and pies, the monks make brittles, truffles, buttercreams, and even the occasional labor-intensive pie. The Jampot's tiny storefront, crowded with visitors during the warmer months of the year, is a miniature cornucopia of sweets and berry-derived delights, full of color and life. "[Truffles] are relatively new," Father Basil says. "We took one of the smaller rooms that are attached here, and we insulated it and climate controlled it, and [use] dehumidifiers when necessary . . . and we invested in a marble slab table so that we can seriously get into the candies. One of the monks devotes himself almost entirely to candy."

And the truffle operation is no joke. The monk in charge worked with serious intensity as we watched, turning out simple but delicious chocolates that would stand up with product sold in any urban area in the state. While the monastic life is meant to provide seclusion, the business side of the operation lets the monks maintain at least a tenuous connection to the concerns and worries of the local lay-folk. By employing locals to pick berries for their jams, Father Basil and his fellow monks get to see life from a perspective sometimes very different from their own.

"Many of them have very interesting takes on things," he says. "We also get derelicts who are just picking enough to get their next bottle of wine, but the serious pickers are very interesting folks."

Jampot Bakery, 6500 Michigan 26, Eagle Harbor. www.societystjohn.com

OTHER EXPERIENCES ALONG THE UPPER PENINSULA

RALPH'S ITALIAN DELI

U.S. Highway 41, Ishpeming (across from the Ski and Snowboard Hall of Fame).
www.ralphsitaliandeli.com

This humble deli with a fifty-plus-year history is one of the best spots to experience unvarnished, old-school UP Italian food in its most primal form. The house specialty is cudighi, and it comes all sorts of ways—mild, medium, or hot, with optional pizza sauce, mushrooms, green peppers and/or giardinera. Turkey cudighi is an option for the slightly more health-conscious visitor. The shop also features a "Where has all the cudighi gone . . . ?" map studded with pins that trace the movements of this signature UP food throughout the United States. They cluster heavily in the Midwest, but make their way to Mexico, Canada, California, up and down the East Coast, and even over-seas, as noted by handmade labels.

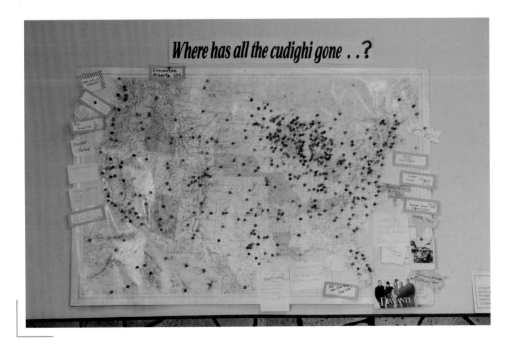

At Ralph's Italian Deli in Ishpeming, a map marks the whereabouts of its signature dish, cudighi.

CLYDE'S

3 U.S. 2, St. Ignace

The lakeside drive-in known as Clyde's in St. Ignace is distinguished by classic road-side burgers—simple and charred with a soulful bun that's neither too bready nor too dense. But its milkshake is probably worth the drive from wherever you call home. It's thick, rich, and deeply flavored, with a clean dairy finish. Clyde's has been open since 1949 and has evolved into a local mini-chain, with locations in Sault Ste. Marie, Michigan, and Manistique, Michigan. Beyond its shakes, it's hailed for its Big C three-quarter-pound burger.

GOETZ'S LOCKVIEW RESTAURANT

329 West Portage Avenue, Sault Ste. Marie

The nautically themed Lockview Restaurant should be your go-to for handmade wooden boats in the style of the big ships that ply Lake Superior—its gift shop is one of the best on the lake. It's also home to a fine breakfast, featuring ham rich with pork flavor (and neither over- or undersalted, in our experience) and chewy, almost crepe-like pancakes with beautifully crisp edges. Goetz's Lockview may also be the only restaurant on the lake to publish its own newspaper; when we visited, we picked up issue number one from the paper's tenth volume, which had details about Sault Ste. Marie, "Michigan's first city," an ad for the Longships Motel next door, and a thorough printing of the restaurant's breakfast, lunch, and dinner menus.

ELIZABETH'S CHOP HOUSE

113 South Front Street, Marquette. www.elizabethschophouse.com

Anywhere there's a university, there tends to be a restaurant custom-made for wining and dining the out-of-town (and often international) visitors who come to town in waves to apply for faculty positions, visit their sons and daughters, and scout the school for prospective attendees. In Marquette, Elizabeth's Chop House seemed to be the place to be. It's a smartly appointed, chic waterfront restaurant that specializes in steaks and chops, plus the likes of escargot, oysters, crab cakes, and a number of other dishes that evoke a seafood feel without necessarily relating to the large body of water lapping at the restaurant's back door. Scan the seafood menu long enough, however, and you'll find a cedar-planked whitefish with garlic spinach and merlot reduction, which was among our favorite preparations of this fish that we tasted during our travels.

HARBOR HAUS

57 First Street, Copper Harbor. www.harborhaus.com

When the ferry from Isle Royale comes in, the waitresses from the Harbor Haus go out—you'll be temporarily without service as the staff of the restaurant dances a high-kicking number to welcome the boat back to the peninsula. This sort of restaurant in this sort of location can be a tourist trap, but we had a terrific meal, crowned by a lovely, properly cooked duck breast with lingonberries and reduced veal jus. The skin was crispy; the meat was tender and rich and complemented beautifully by the tart berries. A smashingly bold, soufflé-like raspberry cobbler was a graceful finish to the meal.

NORTH STAR LOUNGE AT THE LANDMARK INN

230 North Front Street, Marquette. thelandmarkinn.com

At times the lonely remoteness of Lake Superior is palpable, but the Landmark Inn evokes the exact reverse. It's a monument to civilization built of fireplaces, high ceilings, and tasteful early-twentieth-century-inspired decor. The comfort of urban life practically oozes from the hotel's dark wood paneling, a throwback to its origin as the Northland Hotel, which opened in 1930. Guests have included Amelia Earhart, Abbott and Costello, and Duke Ellington. Head up to the North Star Lounge on the sixth floor, and relax by the fireplace with a single malt scotch in your hand—this is, no doubt, a slice of what it was like to be a timber or copper baron back in the day.

THE ANTLERS

804 East Portage Avenue, Sault Ste. Marie. www.saultantlers.com

You want local color? The Antlers, a bar and restaurant in Sault Ste. Marie, has got it. The restaurant was originally called the "The Bucket of Blood Saloon" and fronted as an ice cream parlor during Prohibition. Emphasizing the connection between animals and food is newly chic thanks to the farm-to-table movement, but The Antlers takes it several steps further by loading down its dining room with dozens (perhaps hundreds?) of taxidermied carcasses and, yes, racks of antlers of all shapes and sizes. From the prosaic (deer) to the exotic (a massive snapping turtle skull), there's something to please everyone, presuming that everyone likes preserved animal remains. While we were at The Antlers, we tried the fried bluegill basket, a rare treat—not many restaurants bother to catch and clean these little fish. The bluegills were lightly breaded, almost sweet in flavor, not at all fishy, a bit lemony and fresh.

WISCONSIN'S SOUTH SHORE

THE GATHERING PLACE

Near [Iron River] is an old railroad station named Winneboujou for a deity of the Chippewa Indians, a roving god who guarded the Chippewa from enemies and occasionally administered a rough and impulsive justice. The forge of this gigantic blacksmith was supposed to be [some] twenty miles to the south, where he fashioned native copper into weapons. Much of his forging was done by moonlight, and the ringing blows of his hammer were heard by Indians along the entire shore of Lake Superior.

The WPA Guide to Wisconsin

OUR POPULAR UNDERSTANDING OF HISTORY in the Upper Midwest seems to stop somewhere around the Civil War. Vague knowledge of Native American settlements and westward-bound settlers fills in the blanks, but everything tends to get fuzzy somewhere in the early nineteenth century. It may therefore be surprising to learn how far back the story of European settlement goes on the South Shore: the Jesuit mission of La Pointe du Saint Esprit was established in 1665 near Washburn on the southwest shore of Chequamegon Bay, a name that was later passed on to the settlement of La Pointe on Madeline Island.

Perhaps it's the layers of history (Plano, Dakota, Ojibwa, French, British, American, and so forth), or perhaps it's the temperate shelter of the Apostle Islands, but there's something about the South Shore that feels more gentle and welcoming than the rest of this wild and often stark lake. Certainly as we sat in Big Water Coffee Roasters in Bayfield sipping lattes, eating impeccable granola served with local milk from Tetzner's Dairy, and reading the *New York Times* Web site on our laptops, we felt closer to cosmopolitan urban life than we may have felt anywhere else around the lake. And the fact that apples can be grown with such success on the South Shore is certainly evidence of a kinder, gentler side of the lake, at least in terms of the weather.

Politically liberal and in touch with seasonal and organic produce, the area has a hippie vibe at times. Madeline Island could well be the epicenter for this feeling. It could be residual energy from the island's history as the spiritual center of the Lake Superior Ojibwa, whose great spirit told the people to travel west to where the "food grows upon the water," leading to the discovery of wild rice growing in the marshes of Chequamegon Bay, or it could just be the general vibe emanating from Tom's Burned Down Café.

The café itself is a natural gathering place for those drawn to the South Shore's natural beauty and slow-paced way of life. In the warmer months, it attracts the kind of free-flowing outdoor party scene that is more typically associated with the Caribbean than northern Wisconsin. If you're drawn to the South Shore, you're probably ultimately drawn to the Apostle Islands, those semiwild outposts just off the shore of Bayfield, and Tom's is the unofficial capital of this place, reflecting a love of strong spirits and warm camaraderie.

Forget the great Wisconsin beer selection, the quirky service, or the legitimately committed party vibe. The real appeal of Tom's Burned Down Café is the building

Pilings from an abandoned Chicago & North Western rail line litter the shore at Ashland.

North woods and south seas meet at Tom's Burned Down Café on Madeline Island.

itself—or lack thereof. The café operates as a forty-foot trailer plus decks plus an open-air bar within a legitimate ruin, the aftermath of a fire in 1992. Potbelly stoves stave off some of the chill during the more ambiguously warm months (May, September, and so forth), and shots of schnapps take care of the rest; in warmer months, the bar crowds up with jolly refugees from the workaday world and is filled with the sound of live music.

Unlike on some of the flintier, wilder parts of the lake, serious food lovers will quite easily find a lot to love on the South Shore. Here nature's bounty has been fully welcomed into the modern gastronomic world, and while you'll miss some of the raw wildness of the Keweenaw or rugged beauty of Rossport, you'll enjoy the comfort of bed-and-breakfasts, the easy joyousness of the autumn Apple Festival in Bayfield, and the convenience of farmers markets. At places like the South Shore Brewery and Deep Water Grille, you'll find local people who embrace the "eat local" mantra with the passion of new converts, and no shortage of food cultivated nearby to enjoy in the restaurants, the pubs, the cafés, and (if you're fortunate enough to be invited over for supper) the homes of locals.

Summer hours are liberal at Tom's Burned Down Café.

A SIMPLE PLAN

SOUTH SHORE BREWERY, ASHLAND

In Ashland, near the water's edge, sits the South Shore Brewery and the connected Deep Water Grille. The facility makes beer, as its name suggests, but its actual function is closer to that of a communal living room for the city as a whole. And owner and brewer Bo Belanger views the place as the physical manifestation of a crusade to create a new eating and drinking culture on the lake: "We led the way," says Belanger. "Back in 1995, we pushed the envelope—people said, 'You're nuts, you don't know what you're doing.'"

He paints a picture of where food was a bit less than twenty years ago: "People

Brewmaster Bo Belanger of South Shore Brewery in Ashland.

Pale ales, brown ales, and stouts are all available at South Shore Brewery.

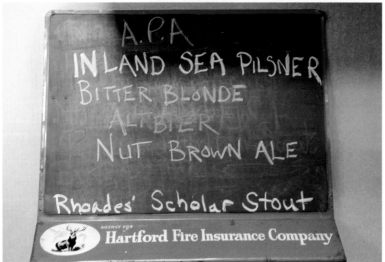

were eating Campbell's soup out of a can back then and saying Bud Light was the best beer ever brewed. We were pushing the envelope back then, and it's always been local. We're growing our own barley and our own hops—it's just a matter of time before it comes to fruition."

Belanger credits the local progressive atmosphere for some of the progress the brewery has made—in contrast to much of rural and particularly suburban Wisconsin, the South Shore is notably liberal in its politics. "Ashland's got two colleges in it, so there are teachers and professionals who are training up, we've got the largest regional hospital [in the area]," says Belanger. "Just that pull has made us a very progressive town. That's how the brewery survives, and the bakery survives, and how the butcher survives—it's because we're a progressive town, we're not a conservative town."

Belanger spent fourteen seasons with the Wisconsin Department of Natural Resources as a fishing biologist, and the Deep Water Grille's menu is (and always has been) adorned with fish. At its old location, before a fire in 2000, the restaurant featured trout cheeks and whitefish livers, two delicacies that locals know and appreciate. "We go out of our way to feature fresh fish," says Belanger. "Come here on a Friday night and we're all about halibut and tuna. When we first came here, nobody would sear tuna. When I first had seared tuna back in the early eighties, I thought 'Oh my God, this is delicious,' but if you tried to tell people that was the way to eat tuna, they'd pooh-pooh you.

"[Local restaurants] have been influenced by what we've done—they don't have the buffets of scoop and serve anymore. They have microgreens, and everything's local, so that trend has been something . . . it's not a trend any more, it's a wave. What I envision is to take it a step further beyond just getting fresh ingredients to having control over the fresh ingredients, getting into the contracting part of it. That's not going up to a farm and asking what's fresh, it's going up and saying, 'Grow these tomatoes for us.'"

As Belanger talks about his brewery and restaurant—his world, really, a place that he has carved out of the surrounding community

ARTESIAN WELL WATER FROM MASLOWSKI BEACH IN ASHLAND

Evaluating the taste of water is a subjective art, particularly when you're comparing a perfectly potable product, Minneapolis tap water, for example, with one reputed to be excellent: water from the beachside artesian well at Ashland's Maslowski Beach.

But here goes: Ashland's artesian water tasted soft, mellow, and almost sweet by comparison to the Minneapolis stuff. If you find yourself in Ashland (or Cornucopia, which has a similar well), make sure you avail yourself of the free public fountain and decide whether you think it was worth the effort.

with as much deliberate focus as a sculptor carving rock—you can practically feel the intensity and integrity sweating out of him. He's fluent in the language of locavore, articulating why a loaf of bread baked by your neighbor made from wheat harvested one county over is necessarily better than a load that came off a truck from an industrial bakery in Philadelphia. It's not that the bread tastes better—but of course, it will—it's that the bread is part of a tightly woven tapestry of relationships, and those relationships, taken together, are the very thing that defines a community. By brewing local beer and cooking with local fish, and by cooking fish in that beer, and knowing the people who grow the barley and catch the fish, Belanger has put himself in the middle of a web of friends and colleagues with a common mission: making the South Shore a better place to live, to visit, to eat, to simply be.

The brewery grows (by way of a contract) its own barley for malting (at a malt house in Thunder Bay) and brewing. "I have a farmer who'll come in and have a pint of nut brown and boast that his barley's in the middle of the stuff," says Belanger. He's setting up local hops production, too, in order to compete with West Coast pale ales ("by the time I get my hands on the hops, they're already picked over," Belanger notes).

Referring to his chef, Kevin Cousins, Belanger says, "I'm a brewer, he's a chef, we're not supposed to be in the commodities market . . . but you hear that yellow peppers are going to skyrocket next week, so you'd better buy a pile right now." On the beer side, the brewery was set up to be English-style, crafting ales (including the flagship Nut Brown), but soon Belanger's passion for lager came up and broadened the brewery's offerings.

A film shot in Ashland in 1998 helped push the brewery over the top in terms of identity and local acceptance. Sam Raimi's *A Simple Plan* starred Billy Bob Thornton and Bill Paxton, and the film crew's sophisticated tastes turned out to be a major windfall for the then-struggling brewpub. "At that point we'd just opened our doors, and we weren't packin' 'em in, so to speak," says Belanger. "We were the closest place [to where Bridget Fonda and Billy Bob Thornton were staying], so they came to the restaurant, and that drew the locals. When they started sitting down at our table and drinking our beer and eating our food, people started saying, 'Oh, this can't be half bad!'"

LOCAVORE ON THE SOUTH SHORE

DEEP WATER GRILLE, ASHLAND

Brewing and cooking are different branches of the same art, and so the cuisine at Deep Water Grille is unsurprisingly deeply influenced by the beer served at the brewery, which serves as the closest thing the area has to a local beer short of "something out of Minneapolis or Leinenkugel's" according to Deep Water Grille chef Kevin Cousins. But that doesn't mean the brewery's craft beer is universally enjoyed.

"There are still people who say, 'I can't afford to eat at your restaurant,' or 'I don't like that beer, it's too dark' or 'it's too heavy,'" says Cousins. "Bo makes beer that's golden blond, and they say it's too dark. They're afraid to trade their Busch Light cans for something new, and they'd be pleasantly surprised."

Cousins riffs off of Belanger's product when he cooks, using the beer as a culinary launching pad. "We make a beer cheese soup that calls for two gallons [of nut brown ale] at a time. There's six gallons of stock, two gallons of beer, and a gallon of cream,"

Chef Kevin Cousins of the Deep Water Grille in Ashland.

says Cousins. "People who have tried to make it at home ask, 'What do you do to make it so good?' And I say, 'You've gotta use a shitload of nut brown! Go heavy on the beer!' We use a cheese that's good, a sharp cheddar. It's all about the ingredients. If you're making your beer cheese soup with Budweiser, it never will compare."

For Cousins, the restaurant—and its use of beer as a culinary element—is about changing the way people eat on the South Shore, "taking the meat and potatoes diet and sort of twisting it up, serving meat and potatoes but not in the same style that they're used to and using a lot of beer. We use it in marinades, we use it in sauces (our barbecue sauce), our beer cheese soup, from everything from pale ale caramelized onions . . . I'll take the nut brown and reduce it with garlic until it's a syrup and put it on meat—just a spoonful of it on meat, and people are like 'wow,' you know."

As part of Cousins's gastronomic mission, he stopped ordering ground pepper, a seemingly minor move that he says has had major repercussions. "We're going to order a couple of twenty-dollar spice grinders, and if you want pepper, you're going to grind it," he recalls. "Something like that, that one little change . . . and yet pepper is used in all the recipes, so that one little change can just boost your menu. Choosing to make that change and realizing that the results are incredible."

Belanger deserves much of the credit for the final meal that ends up on diners' plates, says Cousins: "It's basically taking all of his hard work and putting it in a pot and reducing it and people go 'wow, Kevin, this is really good!' Well, he did all the work."

He credits his democratically run kitchen, as well: the staff talks about the food, tastes the food, and argues about the food in their search for the finished recipe. "That's why the menu sells so well," says Cousins. "If the majority of the kitchen staff likes it a certain way, it's true in the dining room too. I encourage them to watch the Food Network, to watch trends, getting five or six different brewing or cooking magazines and handing them out. I'll say, I have buffalo hanger steaks in there, get on the Internet and figure out what to do with them. It's about keeping that excitement and drive going. Showing them that cooking can be a lot of fun and really rewarding."

Before we left the brewpub, Cousins whipped up an off-the-menu dish he called "beer blanc" whitefish, a play off of the traditional "beurre blanc" butter sauce that is a staple of French cuisine. "What I did here is I took our Lake Superior fresh whitefish, it's never frozen here, and I dusted it with a little cornmeal and salt and pepper and

"Beer blanc" is a buttery whitefish prepared at the Deep Water Grille.

then I panfried it in some clarified butter and took it out of the pan and threw a few vegetables in there: some cherry tomatoes, some asparagus, and squash. And then I took the vegetables out the pan and deglazed the pan with some Inland Sea Pilsener and a little bit of chicken stock and then let that reduce, and then added some cold butter . . . and so it's kind of like a beer beurre blanc, and then it was served with a little lemon basil risotto."

The dish is profoundly rich, buttery, balanced, and lively in flavor thanks to the textural and flavor contrast of the risotto. Cousins points up the unexpected parallel between lobster and whitefish: "If you've been to different areas of the world where lobster is the delicacy or crabmeat, here whitefish is the delicacy. I compare cooking whitefish to cooking paper—it's so thin, once you heat up the outside of it, the inside is going to get hot. I basically cooked it for thirty seconds in a hot pan, flipped it and cooked it for thirty more seconds, and it was done."

South Shore Brewery and Deep Water Grille, 808 Main Street West, Ashland, 715-682-4200. www.southshorebrewery.com

Co-owners Mary Dougherty and Renee Teeter stand outside Good Thyme Restaurant in Washburn.

YAPPY HOUR AT THE BOAT BAR

GOOD THYME RESTAURANT, WASHBURN

"It's so different over here [on the South Shore]," says Mary Dougherty. Dougherty co-owns the Good Thyme Restaurant near Washburn. It's a magnificent old house on a sprawling piece of property that feels like a slice of country opulence. "It's not as austere as it is on the North Shore," says Dougherty, whose feelings about the land— and her livelihood—are passionate and voluminous. "How it looks, your access to the lake is different. When you're up in Grand Marais or Lutsen, you've got this big hill— this rocky, intense, formidable coast. Here, you're tucked in by the islands. You know you're on a big body of water, but there is much easier access, most of the beaches are sandy—it has a whole different feel. It feels more like . . . the North Shore seems like a place that is more touristy. I feel like people live here."

"I can't leave the lake," says co-owner Renee Teeter. "I grew up here, and when I moved away, I couldn't stand it. When I came back, it was for family, but it was also for the lake. I don't care if I just see it during the day . . . I know it's there. I don't think we'd survive without it, because it brings our customers. That's what we have in common: the lake. We always had a boat, every weekend we'd go out on the lake [in Washburn]."

"The Apostle Islands were just designated one of Wisconsin's seven natural wonders," notes Dougherty. "Because the lake is—when you are by that body of water, you are in the presence of something primal."

"Years ago when my dad was a teacher, we'd go hang out on the docks or by the fishermen, and we'd hang out on our boat," recalls Teeter. "It was not like it is today. It was like the Keweenaw when I was young. They haven't really been touched yet. There's those old stores . . . you don't get any more local than me, because my ancestors were here on the frontier." Growing up, local food for Teeter meant wild rice, venison, and fish. And for greens? "As a kid we'd always pick wild leeks and do the wild rice . . . we're big on the leeks, they're all along the riverbeds here," she says.

The hundred-year-old building that houses Good Thyme has a storied past. It used to be a farmhouse on a thousand-acre farm owned by a lumber baron/banker and a schoolteacher. "So they had a mile and a half of lakeshore, including Houghton Falls," says Dougherty. "And then he died about three years after it was built, and she sold it back to the lumber company. People say it was a brothel—and it wasn't really a brothel. It was a bar and rooming house. What are they going to do if they want to keep their guys' paychecks? Throw 'em some women and some booze. It was more like a company store."

The restaurant has stayed steady in its intent since its founding in 2001 and relocation to its current location after a fire: good local food, booze, and hospitality. "You have to be very present all the time," says Dougherty. "I came in here on Sunday with my family to have dinner, I walk in and I know people, I'm giving them hugs, I'm so happy to see them there. Feeding people is a really intimate thing, and you have to be aware of that—and we both are."

The food that Good Thyme serves is part sophisticated urban fare, part traditional lake food—sometimes mussels and wine, sometimes meatloaf, sometimes puff pastry and potatoes. When we visited, the menu included everything from wood-fire grilled steak and Mongolian pork tenderloin to chicken saltimbocca to Lake Superior trout picata to Thai peanut salad. "We have local fish," says Dougherty. "We belong to a CSA out in Ashland. We try to get as much local stuff as we can. It's challenging up here, because there isn't the same infrastructure buildup as a large city might have. Everyone's on the locavore thing, but that's just how we eat up here, we're really isolated."

That isolation, however, doesn't stop Good Thyme's owners from stocking and serving the good stuff. The bar selection is impressive—Kelt cognac next to Buffalo Trace bourbon next to a swath of intriguing top-shelf stuff—with makings for cocktails like the Old Fashioned Good Thyme (Clear Creek brandy from Oregon, top-flight Luxardo maraschino cherries, and Fee Brothers bitters) and the Teddy Tini (Hendrick's Gin, Dolin Dry Vermouth, and Lindsay natural green olives).

That said, it's the wine cellar downstairs that is downright enchanting for a lover of spirits. "Wine to me is like magic," Dougherty says. "The person who is in the vineyard . . . they come up in their head what they want it to taste like, they put it in the barrel . . . they have no idea. It's like Aladdin's lamp every time I open a bottle of wine—it unleashes where they picked it, what the weather was like, and what they were hoping for at that time. It's like alchemy, when you're working with something that evolves in the environment."

From Dougherty's perspective, it's fortunate that there's a palpable sense of wonder that comes along with food and drink—it's part of what makes the gig endur-

able and enjoyable. "A lot of my compensation does not come from money," she says. "If I was just in it for the money, I'd be very depressed. I'd be out of here already. But there is something with . . . when you walk in, and people signed on to your gig. They're here to spend their money and time, and they're willing to bring friends in, and they trust us enough to make their recommendation be a hit—that's a huge compliment. We have to keep our sights set on that."

Part of that sense of fun is reflected in Good Thyme's "Yappy Hour," a weekly gathering (during warm weather) of dogs and owners at the restaurant's boat bar, a (profoundly) beached boat that has been turned into an outdoor bar. "In another life, I so want to run a dog day care," Dougherty says. "I can't do that, but I'm a good bartender, and I like dogs. So we have a boat bar out there, so I run my dogs in, and they help me bartend and bark at things. It's fun! Sometimes guest dogs can come in and guest bartend if they get along with my dogs. It's just something that makes me happy."

Good Thyme Restaurant, 77180 Highway 13, Washburn, 715-373-5255. goodthymerestaurant.com

THE APPLES OF THE NORTH

BAYFIELD APPLE COMPANY, BAYFIELD

"Bayfield" and "apples" are synonymous to nearly anyone familiar with this pretty little lakeside town. Known as the gateway to the scenic Apostle Islands in Lake Superior, Bayfield is also the center of northwestern Wisconsin's apple cropping and home to an annual apple festival that brings an estimated 40,000 people to this city of 530 people.

The secret to Bayfield's success as a producer of fruit is the climate, which is mellower than that of other locales in northern Wisconsin. "The lake and the [Apostle] islands have created a microclimate," says Steve Hoekstra of the Bayfield Apple Company. "[Nearby town] Cornucopia's not quite as good, Washburn's not quite as good. There's a one-mile by four-mile area right here that is a microclimate. We're a [plant hardiness] zone 4 here. We're on the tip of Wisconsin, and most people would say, 'You should be a zone 5 or zone 6.'"

"I've got friends in the Twin Cities who ask, 'How can you grow apples that far north?'" says Hoekstra. The answer is the surrounding water of the lake and its consistent (relative) warmth of thirty-eight degrees. "The islands protect us from the brisk north winds," says Hoekstra. "Our temperature at night is zero, our temperature during the day is twenty-five to thirty-five. Every day in the winter it's ten to fifteen degrees warmer here than it is in the Twin Cities, and we get 150 to 180 inches of snow. And it doesn't get unbearably hot in the summer; we have a gradual warm-up. That's what's created this."

Bayfield Apple
Company owner
Steve Hoekstra
and his son.

Hoekstra took over the Apple Company in 2010, three weeks before the apple festival. "My wife said if I ever did that again, she will leave me," he says, only half kidding. "It was a very difficult three-week period." Hoekstra and his son run the orchard, and they take care to treat their cider with ultraviolet light rather than pasteurizing it. "I have tons of people buying cider from us in bulk to make their own apple wine, because we don't pasteurize, so it will ferment," he says. The farm has fifteen productive varieties of fruit and trees that date back more than 125 years, to the early waves of the area's European settlers.

CRANBERRY APPLE PIE AT JUDY'S GOURMET GARAGE

Judy's Gourmet Garage, 85130 Highway 13, Bayfield, 715-779-5365

Judy's Gourmet Garage is the best not-kept nonsecret on the lake, a garage turned into a full-on pie shop. The cranberry apple pie was killer: the flaky and tender crust could have won a contest, and the filling was pleasingly firm and a great balance between sweet and tart, cranberry versus apple. A cinnamon-spiked crust was an added bonus. This pie does not simply triumph over a Betty's pie (referring to the former mandatory-stop pie shop near Two Harbors on Minnesota's North Shore)—it buries a Betty's pie.

The turnovers may be even better than the pies. A blueberry turnover had a great sweetly spiced kick, delicate pastry, cream cheese frosting, and filling that walked the line between too austere and plain and too sweet and artificial.

When you take a moment to stand outside in the orchard at Bayfield Apple Company, you're struck by the fact that you're not just in some sort of outdoor factory that creates fruit for the marketplace. You're also standing in a horticultural library, where the books are trees, and the words are the genetic material of each individual breed represented on-site. The existence of independent orchards and farms allows for the retention of biological memory in the form of breeds of trees (or grain, or other food crops) that might not have immediate commercial utility but could prove crucial later on after climate change, or plant disease, or insect predation has changed the shape of the playing field for growers and their crops.

But diversity aside, two apple varieties really drive the bulk of the orchard's commerce. "People like you, from the Twin Cities, come and I call them H customers—they're looking for Haralsons or Honeycrisps," Hoekstra says. "If we don't have 'em, we can't convince them to buy any other kind of apples. Here's the thing with Honeycrisp, is that there's such demand for them ... we sold the number ones. We bagged up and sold seconds. We had thirds that were not good enough to go into bags, and we dumped them on the table ... and those sold. Of 210 bushels of [Honeycrisp] apples we had maybe 5 bushels not good enough for people to buy. That's impacted our business. The week before Apple Fest, we were the only ones up here who still had Honeycrisp."

The frenzy for the Honeycrisp, a variety of apple developed in 1960 by the University of Minnesota and released in 1991, famed for its firmness and sweetness, is such that other growers sometimes cross the line in an effort to meet market demand. "I have neighbors—and I'm not going to say who—who, because of that frenzy, are selling another variety of apple as Honeycrisp," says Hoekstra. "Some of the older people, the fifth generation, still believe you can sell crap to tourists and they'll buy it. They don't realize they're Internet savvy. I have to chuckle when someone comes in from down the road and tries our Honeycrisp and says, 'Well, that doesn't taste like the Honeycrisp your neighbor has.' My neighbor doesn't have any Honeycrisp. I know that for a fact."

Hoekstra has a few words of advice for those who want their apples to last: "If you take care of an apple, it will last for eight months. Apples are like humans: they like skin-to-skin contact, only they like it at thirty-eight degrees. If you leave 'em in the bushel box ... you can hold them in a suspended state.

Apples in storage at the Bayfield Apple Company.

"We sell them in plastic bags with vent holes. When you take them home, you keep them in that bag at thirty-six or thirty-eight degrees at 80 percent humidity, they would still be good eight months from now."

Hoekstra's orchard makes its own pectin for its jam and cuts back on beet sugar in its jam recipes as a result. "Our product is the envy of the industry because if you look at it, it's fruit, fruit, fruit, fruit, a little bit of sugar, some spices," he says. "You don't see fructose, you don't see all the crap . . . it's got a three-year shelf life, unopened."

The orchard grows an older variety of the much-maligned Red Delicious apples. But unlike some bigger producers, Hoekstra doesn't stabilize the apples with CO_2 in massive, Quonset hut–like structures. "You will find that these Red Delicious have a better flavor," says Hoekstra. "They're a whole lot different than the ones you'll find in the grocery store." Indeed, the apples have a deeper flavor and firmer texture than their grocery-store equivalents, a testament to how mass marketing can compromise flavor and texture in the name of economy and shelf stability.

Bayfield Apple Company, 87540 County Highway J, Bayfield, 715-779-5700. www.bayfieldapple.com

A WALK IN THE WOODS

SASSY NANNY FARMSTEAD CHEESE, HERBSTER

Not far from the South Shore of Lake Superior, on a woodsy plot of land in the country, there lives a goatherd. Once upon a time (or once upon a place, for that matter), this wasn't an unusual profession, but in northern Wisconsin in the modern era, Michael Stanitis and his goats stand out. "Every night I make a big stiff cocktail and head out down the road and into the woods with them, and that's the way it used to be done," says Stanitis. "There's a reason that people were shepherds and herders—the most natural way to feed your animals is to let them eat what they want to eat." (Whether goatherds in the 1400s would regularly make "a nice gin and tonic" or mango margarita before taking their goats for a constitutional is a topic best left to medieval historians, but there's no denying that it's a slower pace of life than what's endured by most of modern America.)

Michael Stanitis of Sassy Nanny Farmstead Cheese in Herbster.

Stanitis, a chef by trade, started building his country home around the year 2000. He'd been working in a café at Franklin and Pillsbury Avenues in Minneapolis and considering a transition to the country life. "I'd spent some summers up here, and I spent winters in the Southwest," he recalls. "I'd cooked on Madeline Island, at a couple different restaurants there. So I was starting to look at what I could do up here and stay in food . . . and really, there's no work here. There's seasonal work, but you have to leave in the winter and be a gypsy."

Stanitis grew up on a farm with goats, and he added together the country property, the need for year-round work, and the possibility of goat cheese and came up with a formula for a new life. In 2008, he started seriously investigating the idea of making cheese for a living. "I made tons of cheese, and every friend I had ate it," he says. "And I kept doing that. I started thinking about getting really serious about it two years ago, and got into the logistics of starting a cheese plant, and getting a cheesemaker's license, and realize how much money, and time . . . it's insane . . . it's unbelievable."

The red tape and expense slowed Stanitis down but didn't stop him. "I can say now being into it for almost a year, I used to make fun of rich people who started restaurants and had never worked in a restaurant a day in their lives. Well, I'm not rich, but I can tell you that the fantasy of having a herd of goats, milking them, making cheese, and marketing the cheese is nonstop work . . . I will know in three years whether it's even worthwhile doing."

THE PROOF IS IN THE CHEESE

Stanitis makes a range of cheeses, including Lake Effect, a fresh, spreadable goat cheese with a clean, bright flavor; Buttin Heads, a sea salt–brined, raw-milk feta; and Cabra Fresco, a soulful homage to queso fresco. The recent construction of a cheese-aging room has allowed Stanitis to begin producing Winey Kid, an aged, raw-milk cheese with a red wine–washed rind; and Finit Sur La Paille, a French-style, moldy rind, aged soft cheese.

Most of the work of creating these cheeses—with everything that comes with that surprisingly Herculean task—comes naturally to Stanitis, but there are still bits of the job that he's figuring out. "I do really enjoy 90 percent of it," he says, before singling out his least favorite aspect of the work. "I can't stand sitting at farmers markets. It makes me want to put an ice pick through my eye. If I have to answer one more fucking question about goats. . . . There are Web sites out there to read about goats, go out there and read about it. I'm not interested in regurgitating it *one more time*."

Stanitis milks about twenty goats, all of which are named colorfully, including a Donatella Versace and a Delilah. He makes about forty to fifty pounds of cheese a week—a fair amount for a single-person artisan operation but not even a drop in the bucket for even a medium-sized commercial cheese plant. "It's seven days a week, ten months a year," he says. "I'm going to milk through November, and then I'll take December and January off. I'm up and I milk and that takes two to three hours with clean up . . . then every three days it's off to the cheese plant to make cheese, and every day I'm there doing something with the cheese . . . and then deliveries, and book work . . ."

Locals are enjoying the product, however. He notes that "the IGA in Washburn is

Buttin' Heads goat cheese is one of a range of cheeses available from Sassy Nanny.

selling shit-tons of my cheese. Shit-tons! Rosie at the deli counter will call and say, 'Hey, can I get twenty pounds of cheese?' and I'm like, 'Shit yeah you can get twenty pounds, that's a lot of money!'"

Stanitis identifies Sassy Nanny's advantage as its small size and forage-driven product. "If people are going to take an extra four or five dollars out of their pocket and spend it on my cheese, they're doing it because they know me and they drive by my farm and see the goats outside in their manger, or they see them out walking with me, and they say, 'Hey, let's give our money to Michael.'"

If you're looking for a symbol of what Lake Superior food means—or can mean, at the very least—it would be hard to do better than the nighttime walk of a shepherd cheesemaker, cocktail in hand, threading his way through the natural world with a pack of four-legged friends at his side. Every night that Stanitis is out there with his goats and his gin and tonic is a victory for those of us who imagine a romantic side to this sometimes brutal lake.

THE PLACE GOATS CALL HOME

"They have a pretty sweet deal," Stanitis says of his goats. "Their house is as big as my house, they're dry, they're well fed. I do most of the work. I clean their house. I do it all! They just have to show up and be tolerable and produce the milk, and I pretty much cover all the other bases for them. They don't have it bad at all. I think you have a responsibility—when you domesticate an animal and you're feeding yourself that way, then I think you have a responsibility to do that."

Stanitis and his goats are helping to change food culture on the South Shore, but it's a movement he sees as already being well underway. "This is not a hotbed of haute cuisine, but that's really changing a lot," he says. "It's so surprising to see my parents' generation showing up at farmers markets to buy beautiful vegetables. And the Sauters [of Spirit Creek Farm] down the road do kimchi . . . and there's Pasture Perfect Poultry in Mason . . . so there's this network of people coming together to provide stuff."

Making food locally can lead to more expensive and irregularly available food, but it's also food that you know a neighbor has labored over—and accountability is as quick as a phone call or visit. "The product may be a little better in that I have

A curious goat at Sassy
Nanny Farmstead Cheese.

complete control over everything," he says. "People who the thought of eating goat cheese makes them shudder, I'll sample them my cheese, and I'm not exaggerating, 90 percent of the time they'll be happy and even buy some. It's all milk quality—you need to feed the animals really well, you need to care for them well, and you need to chill the milk right away.

"Because specifically goat milk has a casein, a protein where when that starts to break down, that's where you get that goaty flavor. Now, I like the goaty flavor in a bucheron or something aged and delicious. But not everybody does. But I did my homework—I'm not going to sell a ton of goaty-tasting cheese up here."

"Goaty" or not, Stanitis's cheese trades on its terroir, or sense of place, imparted by the air, the soil, and the plants that the goats feed on. That doesn't stop him from being skeptical about some of the finer points of terroir, however; that is, whether a specific plant or soil really has a palpable, discernable impact on the end product. "It's not something you can taste or smell or touch—it's like going home," he says. "It's this feeling that ties you to something. My goats walk through these woods every night, and they eat a little balsam, and a little blackberry, and they eat a little bit of this and a little bit of that . . . Is it really going to distinguish that cheese? I think it'll make for better milk, because they're selecting fresh greenery . . . Can you really quantify that and qualify that?"

That said, he notes: "I like doing what I do here because people used to do it here. There was a cheesemaker in the town of Cornucopia. There was a cheesemaker between Port Wing and Iron River on County A. There's even a road called Cheese Factory Road. For me, the sense of place is about bringing something back to the place that used to exist." That sense of place extends to Lake Superior, in a profound way. "I lived in Duluth for a few years," he says. "I just saw the lake, and I loved it. I'm hooked on the lake. There's just something about Lake Superior. I grew up in eastern Pennsylvania and spent a lot of time on the Eastern Seaboard and New England, and even the ocean didn't get me in the same way that Lake Superior did."

"I think there's something to be said for the things we innately do to promote our survival," he says. "We're never going to be without water, that's really a great thing. You do have to like the winter, though. That's part of it."

Sassy Nanny Farmstead Cheese is available in markets throughout the South Shore; for more information, visit www.sassynanny.com

FROM MEAD TO BRACKETTS

WHITE WINTER WINERY, IRON RIVER

Ask a food lover—even one who is well informed—whether there's an Upper Midwestern stand-in for port wine as an after-dinner drink, and they may well come up empty. But the remarkable fortified Black Harbor—a black currant honey wine with neutral spirits added to bring this complex yet pleasingly sweet beverage up to 21 percent alcohol by volume—is a gorgeous stand-in and a suitable wingman for blue cheese, nutty desserts, and anything else that normally calls for a European dessert wine as an accompaniment.

White Winter, which is based in Iron River, has been in business for more than fifteen years. "On good days, he takes credit for the two hobbies that got us into this, beekeeping and home brewing," says Kim Hamilton, referring to her husband, Jon. "And on bad days, he blames me for letting those hobbies get out of hand."

Jon Hamilton of White Winter Winery in Iron River.

The Hamiltons used to produce the honey that went into their mead (3,600 pounds a year at peak) before the mead operation got too large for their bees. "Beekeeping's been in my family for three generations, so I've always been familiar with mead," says Jon. "It was almost two years of research and development to come up with the recipes."

White Winter is a true locavore operation, from its mission, stated on its Web site ("The Winery was founded on the principles of sustainability and utilization; to use what our region produces to make high quality products and build coalitions and partnerships with growers, producers and other businesses"), to the raw ingredients used to create its meads and other mead family drinks, including bracketts (made with honey and grain), melomels (made with honey and fruit), and metheglins (honey with spices), plus hard ciders and nonalcoholic fruit spritzes.

The beauty of White Winter comes not just from the vaulted space of their two-story, barn-like store and winery in Iron River but also from what their products represent: an old way of drinking and preserving nature's bounty that has largely (but not entirely) faded from consciousness with the dominance of wine and beer as our tableside companions. Just the now-obscure names of the beverages made and sold at White Winter call up an agrarian past, a way to take some of the most locally reflective pieces of fruit, and honey, and grain, and water, and turn them into durable celebration beverages that tell the

PAARYNAT FERMENTED PEAR CIDER FROM WHITE WINTER WINERY

Made from pears grown on the Bayfield peninsula, White Winter's hard pear cider clocks in at a mellow 6.5 percent alcohol by volume and brings a dry, clean maturity to a class of beverage that can often be syrupy and falsely sweet. The flavor of pear strikes the palate most noticeably in the finish of each sip; the body is clean and clear. According to the Hamiltons of White Winter, this cider can be cellared for up to a year. The name Paarynat means "pears" in Finnish.

story of a place. That potential comes through with every sip of their products, which are tart and sweet and honeyed and fruited and effervescent in different proportions from bottle to bottle and glass to glass. The taste of White Winter's beverages is a taste of the South Shore.

"About 95 to 98 percent of our raw ingredients come from within 150 miles of us. We try to keep it local, which is one reason why we don't make grape wines—we don't really grow grapes effectively up here, at least not yet," says Jon. "At that time, there were no grapes available, and I'm a believer of using what's in your own backyard."

The Hamiltons' backyard is a fruitful one, indeed. Beyond the honey, Iron River is in apple county, as it's near to Bayfield. "And we're in one of the premier bramble fruit areas in the country, so the blueberries, the raspberries, the currants all grow really well up here," says Jon.

Wine making has long been a challenge in the Superior region, the development of cold-hardy grapes by the University of Minnesota notwithstanding. "They tend to have a real high acid level and a foxiness. It's hard to make a dry red wine because they have a high acidity," says Jon of cold-climate grapes. "The three parameters for making a good wine are all about balance—balancing the titratable total acidity with the sweetness and the alcohol level. So if you have a real high acid fruit, one of ways to deal with that is to leave a little more sweetness in the finish."

The implications are awesome for the Upper Midwest, if underappreciated: "Theoretically, the Midwest could turn into the port and eiswein capital of the world—those high-acid drinks can taste fabulous," says Jon. "The only way to work with the characteristics of the fruit is to leave that residual sweetness rather than trying to fight it. Currants are a fruit with a really high acid level—primarily citric acid—whereas grapes are malic acid. And you can convert malic acid into a lactic acid, which is much softer and easier to drink. But you can't do that with black currants, so there's not a real effective way to deal with the high acid of currants."

THE HARRY POTTER BOOM

The Hamiltons have a seen a bump in interest in their product in part because of mead's association with the fantasy worlds of Harry Potter and J. R. R. Tolkien's *The*

Lord of the Rings. In part, too, says Jon, a drive toward locavore dining and drinking has spurred interest. "With the economy, people have been hitting the roots," he says. "This is as much roots as you can get, with beverages. People have discovered local food again, and our stuff is pretty local."

And, adds Jon, mead can be a long-term investment. "When we first opened, we'd tell people, drink it in a couple of years," he recalls. "Then as time went on, we realized that was not holding true. We've had stuff now that is fourteen or fifteen years

Several award-winning wines are for sale at White Winter Winery.

old that's unbelievable, like drinking velvet. We've had to change our tune. Honey has natural antiseptic and aging properties. They've found edible honey in Egyptian tombs that's two thousand years old. Fruit wines made with sugar don't age—they just don't hold up. But meads are different."

White Winter Winery, 68323 Lea Street, Iron River, 800-697-2006. whitewinter.com

BREWING BEER IN THE OLD CREAMERY

THIRSTY PAGAN BREWING, SUPERIOR

When Steve Knauss bought Twin Ports Brewing Company in Superior, he promptly changed the name to something a little more controversial: Thirsty Pagan Brewing, a callout to the wild Nordic heritage that is still evident on the shores of Superior.

The decision was no marketing blunder or idle thought. "When we first changed the name, people were like 'Oh my God, you gotta change the name . . . people aren't going to come here,'" recalls owner Steve Knauss. "The reason we picked it is because it was edgy enough to irritate people like that. I told my dad, 'If people don't come here because of the name, we don't want them here in the first place.' In four and a half years, we've had to throw three people out total. We're a bar. In Superior. And we're open in the winter."

Thirsty Pagan is housed in a former creamery, with tiled floors and walls and a peculiar feel to the space that can only be attributed to its former use. Once upon a time in Wisconsin, dairy plants occupied thousands of country crossroads, but consolidation (for better and worse) meant far fewer and often far larger dairy plants. Meanwhile, the old plants were either torn down or reappropriated as housing or space for new businesses—like the Thirsty Pagan.

There's something about the Thirsty Pagan that feels like home. It could be the corkboard trivets that sit beneath the pizzas, or the way the sounds of music and boisterous banter bounce off the tiled walls. It could be the pizzas, which are big and deep and thrown together thoughtfully. It could be that the place once made cheese and now makes beer and pizza—the holy trinity of Wisconsin comfort foods, shrewdly artful and utterly lacking in pretense. Whatever the reason, the place invites investigation, and once you've left, it calls you back.

Steve Knauss of Thirsty Pagan Brewing in Superior.

COCONUT STOUT FROM THIRSTY PAGAN BREWING

Like in any good flavored beer, the dominant added taste (in this case, coconut) in this stout is both clearly present but in balance, asserting itself early but then fading smoothly into the background of the beer. Dark but not heavy, this is a novelty beer that transcends its novelty and stands up as an eminently drinkable delight.

The make process is relatively straightforward, involving real ingredients (as opposed to an extract or artificial flavor). "Our brewer took the coconuts, roasted them in the oven, about fifty pounds worth, and threw them into the mash," says Thirsty Pagan owner Steve Knauss. "Once it goes through the mash, it's fermented in. It's flakes—like oatmeal."

Despite—or perhaps because of—the position his business occupies in the local community, Knauss is happy to speak bluntly about where he lives and works. "Duluth and Superior are kind of a backwater of sadness," he says. "Duluth and Superior have phenomenal performing arts, phenomenal art, and phenomenal people—there simply aren't enough people to appreciate and afford it." But he contrasts his view of the area with his own experience with Thirsty Pagan: "But what happens is you get a place like this. We had to take out the kitchen and the brewery and add seventy seats because we were turning people away. The point is you can't become the bitter northlander."

We ask him why Superior, Wisconsin, is a better place to be located than Duluth, Minnesota. "It probably isn't," Knauss says, bluntly. "Duluth would be a much better place to be. But insurance for this place was $1,800, and it was exactly the same number in Duluth—in Duluth it was every month, in Superior it was every year. Because of the different laws in Minnesota versus Wisconsin, in terms of alcohol. We can't afford that. Why would you do that? Why won't Minnesota sell alcohol on Sunday or in grocery stores? The stupid Lutherans!"

So other than alcohol laws, why have a business in Superior? "[Twin Ports] had a location, it had customers, it had glasses—we opened the door and people came in. The first two years we opened, I was here every day. I was here every day, I was here every night, I was here 110 hours a week, that's what you do. On Father's Day one year, I literally came in, did the bank, did the washing of the building, ordered all the stuff, locked the building, went over to my family, got in the car, drove to the Twin Cities. On the way back, when we got to Cloquet, I realized I'd left the keys in the lock. I was so tired . . . You know who found them? Nobody! It was fine. The place was still locked. That's Superior."

IN, OF, AND FOR THE COMMUNITY

For Knauss, the key to the Thirsty Pagan's livelihood isn't publicity, or tourism, or attaining some artificial standard of pizza excellence. It's the way it relates to its neighbors, its regular customers, and the city of Superior in general.

Few restaurants are more traditional and comfortable in these parts than a beer and pizza joint, but the Thirsty Pagan is a little different, starting with its ingredient source. "The grain we get is from right down the road," says Knauss.

"Everything is as locally purchased as it can get. More than buying locally, we support things made locally. We don't spend money on advertising. I'll sit on the board of directors for local organizations, like the Sister Cities foundation, the Young [Breast Cancer] Survivor Foundation. . . . We'll work with the dog pound, we'll work with the zoo . . . how we advertise is we make those guys happy and they'll come in."

The Thirsty Pagan has become a fixture of the scene, employing two people full-time and another twenty plus part-time. It has eight brews on draft most evenings, typically four rotating specialties and four bedrock go-to brews including North Coast Amber, Whitecap Wheat, Burntwood Black, and Derailed Ale. "Nate [McAlpine] is our brewer, and he brews literally whatever he wants," says Knauss. "I give him that authority, because I want him to take ownership of his position. It's my brewery and my reputation, but I want him to have ownership of his position."

The beer, of course, is a wonderful complement to the Pagan's distinctively heavy, cheesy, pleasantly scorched pizza. "We have quality pizza available every night, and we can deliver it to you on a timely basis. It's kind of funny, it has so many ingredients, you might think you'd lose the pizza in it, but you don't. And it's cooked! It's crunchy on top. People go, 'It's burnt,' but I say, no, taste it, try it."

He's right—we tried the restaurant's "Derailed," a massive sledge of a pie containing eleven toppings (including but not limited to black olives, ham, sausage, and salami). The scorched top is browned, not blackened, and it adds a ton of texture and savory flavor to the pizza—it's definitely a feature, not a bug.

As the brewpub has evolved, it has defied his expectations, becoming more of a family gathering place. The pizza is paramount; the beer plays an important support role. "We thought people would have three to four pints and a pizza and go home.... But people bring their families, have a pint or two, and pizza, then go. When we first bought the place, it was a sausage factory. There weren't women in here for months at a time. Now, you'll come and it'll be not just women in here, but all kinds of women—businesswomen, women who are sixty years old with tattoos on."

The uniting factor is the Pagan's sense of hospitality. There's an ineffable *Cheers*-like quality where you can see regulars are made comfortable. It's not merely a stop for food or a drink—it's a place to hang out. "The people who do come here, their expectations are set. They don't leave in half an hour. They come here and sit for an hour and half. Do you see any TVs? You talk to your people. This room will get pretty loud . . . but you talk. People talk to each other here."

Here he points across the room at a table of four men in their twenties. "You see those guys over there? They all had their cell phones out. I went over to the table and said [and here he bangs on the table], 'Hey! You look like a bunch of middle school girls, put those damn things away.' They went [and here to show their response, he offers up a stunned expression, mouth agape]. 'Don't take 'em out! Talk to each other!' The only time I won't do that is when it's a young kid and they're with their parents. If I see people texting, I'll say, 'Who are you texting? If it's someone you're texting to come here, great, do that and put it away. Otherwise just put it away.'"

Thirsty Pagan Brewing, 1623 Broadway Street, Superior, 715-394-2500.
www.thirstypaganbrewing.com

A deep-dish pizza at Thirsty Pagan Brewing.

SHORE LEAVE IN SUPERIOR

ANCHOR BAR, SUPERIOR

The Anchor Bar is an anomaly in Superior, a gritty port city that, thanks to the international sailors who carouse its streets, has one of the liveliest bar cultures in the state of Wisconsin—a state that itself has one of the liveliest bar cultures in the country, if not the world. It's an old-school beer bar with a modern twist, adapting enough to stay lively without losing its soul in the process.

"My parents bought it in 1977," says co-owner Adam Anderson. "It started as a beer bar, basically. We ended up adding food to it four or five years later."

"This bar in particular used to be a big sailor bar," he recalls. "People would come off the ships and spend their money. I used to hear stories from my dad about the guys coming off the boats.... They'd take their paychecks and come in and gamble for thousands of dollars."

"Before it used to be people from Russia and Belgium coming off the ships," he recalls. "Now, you just don't see them. They used to be from all over the world, and now it's very rare to see someone who doesn't speak English. Before they'd come in: 'Beer.' They'd just know 'beer.'"

That rough-and-ready atmosphere still remains—in part. "It's part of the lore of this place that the service is not the best," says Anderson, grinning. "My manager would say she doesn't know where that came from, but I think it comes from her! Everybody's got their characteristics, I guess."

With the change in shipping—smaller crews and fewer stops in Superior—the sailor traffic to the Anchor has dwindled. "Now it's changed where they're not coming off the boats anymore, they're saving their money to bring home. In that aspect, this middle part of town has gone down because the shipping industry hasn't been as strong."

Anderson and his brother took over in July 2008 after their parents passed away, Anderson (who went to culinary school in the Twin Cities) running the place. A brush with fame via the TV show *Diners, Drive-Ins, and Dives* has bolstered the bar's profile. Fans will drive across the bridge from Duluth because they saw the bar and its famous burgers on TV. "It's the unique atmosphere and the cheap, good food," says Anderson. "That's what it comes down to. We put out a fresh product that's good, and it's very

Adam Anderson, co-owner of the Anchor Bar in Superior.

reasonable for what you get. Without the food here we'd just be a beer bar. All we do is burgers and fresh-cut French fries."

A local butcher grinds the meat for the Anchor's burgers fresh each day, Anderson says. "They bring it in every single day, and if we need more, they'll bring it," he says. "It's really nice, they're local. We get our buns in every day—the buns are made every day, too, in Duluth."

"You get the big food reps like Sysco trying to press their stuff, but my dad kept it local, and so do we," he adds. "But I get our produce from Walmart, because it's cheaper. I'd get it in by the case, but we don't have anywhere to store it."

The bar's fries taste fresh, startlingly redolent of potatoes and little else, a shock to the system for people who are used to saltier, more thoroughly processed products. "When we get an order, we take a potato, send it through the cutter, right into the fryer," says Anderson. "We don't blanch 'em or put 'em in salt water . . . they just go right into the fryer for four and a half or five minutes. That's the way my dad started doing it—if it ain't broke, don't fix it."

Another thing that ain't broke: cheap beer. "Every night after 10:00 P.M. and all day on Monday we do $2.50 pitcher specials," says Anderson. "And it's regularly $2.75 for a thirty-two-ounce mug of beer. We offer eighty-five kinds of beer, with six on draught. We used to only have two when my dad first started." Now the bar offers everything from Summit to Capital Brewing to Sam Adams to Leinenkugel's seasonal offerings. "Tap beer is a whole different ball game," says Anderson.

For some reason, the word that comes to mind when thinking about the Anchor Bar is *encrusted*, the way an old boat or pier becomes encrusted with barnacles, or an anchor resting on the floor of the ocean becomes encrusted with rust and coral. The crust, in the case of this bar–restaurant, is the memories of generation after generation of visitors and the maritime bric-a-brac that gives the place an atmosphere as thick as butter. You don't visit the Anchor, you inhabit it; you feel yourself sinking into the tables and chairs, and the knotted ropes and polished brass of the artifacts that fill the walls. That and a pitcher or three of good cheap beer can make it a difficult place to leave.

THE HAMBURGER AT THE ANCHOR BAR

Three dollars buys you one of the most reliably tasty burgers available in the Lake Superior region. Hand-pattied beef and a satisfying, locally made bakery bun elevate this plainspoken but delicious burger above most of its mass-made brethren, and the value couldn't be better. Despite the Anchor's surge of fame in recent years, its menu is as affordable as you'd hope for in a working-class bar in a port town.

A life ring from the *Edmund Fitzgerald* adorns the wall of the Anchor Bar.

"One neat piece that we have is a life ring from the *Edmund Fitzgerald*, it's hanging on the wall," says Anderson. "There are only supposed to be a couple of them left. We acquired it from someone who said it washed up on the shore. My dad bought it for a couple grand."

"Now people just bring stuff in, and they say, 'Hey, this would look good on your wall,'" he says. That goes both ways, however. "Of course, if it's not bolted down, it'll walk away, so we have to screw everything down."

Anchor Bar, 413 Tower Avenue, Superior, 715-394-9747. anchorbar.freeservers.com

OTHER EXPERIENCES ALONG SUPERIOR'S SOUTH SHORE

BAYFIELD APPLE FESTIVAL

bayfield.org/bayfield-activities/bayfield-apple-festival

Food booths and orchard booths swelling with caramel apples, apple pies, apple tarts, apple bratwurst, and apple cider are just the start of the Bayfield Apple Festival, an annual event that fills this tiny town with tens of thousands of visitors. Art exhibitions, a kids' carnival, craft booths, a "Venetian Boat Parade," live music, performances by the local Ojibwa Drum and Dance Troop, and more shenanigans make the long weekend a merry and apple-tastic time to be in Bayfield. Book your room early if you're planning to stay overnight; accommodations fill up far in advance.

SEA CAVE KAYAKING

www.livingadventure.com/summer

The sandstone sea caves of Lake Superior's Apostle Islands are among the wonders of the U.S. landscape, a place not particularly strapped for wonders. Shaped by wind and water, these haunting caverns invite adventurous visitors to plumb their depths with nimble kayaks, boats perfectly made for the twists and turns of the rock.

If you're lucky, food writer Beth Dooley will be organizing a "Taste of the Apostles" kayak trip around the Bayfield area. Beyond natural beauty, the trip features local food including the likes of honey wine from White Winter, goat cheese from Sassy Nanny, beer from New Glarus, Wisconsin, local bacon, and more. And if you're not fortunate enough to snag a spot in the tour, there's no law against packing your own cooler with the same sort of good stuff. Bayfield has plenty of local gourmet goods available for visitors.

FARMERS MARKETS

200 block of Chapple Avenue, Ashland; Third Street and Mannypenny Avenue, Bayfield;
Bayfield Street, Washburn; under the willows at the beach, Cornucopia.
www.superiorgrown.org/directory/market.htm

Ashland, Bayfield, Washburn, and Cornucopia all have farmers markets during the summer months that make for a deep dip into the world of South Shore food. Talk to a farmer, and you'll be able to figure out the restaurants, value-added foods, and local produce specialties that best represent the bounty of the lake during whatever month or week you happen to be visiting.

RITTENHOUSE INN

301 Rittenhouse Avenue, Bayfield. www.rittenhouseinn.com

Hotels and bed-and-breakfasts can go wrong in a number of ways: too big and impersonal, too small and claustrophobia inducing, too dirty, too stuck in old (and bad) ways of preparing food. The Rittenhouse Inn in Bayfield is that rare, remarkable place that gets the balance right. It's not a place to watch TV and use Wi-Fi—it's a place to relax by a fireplace in a charming classic room and enjoy spectacular views of and access to the lake. It's also home to a remarkably good restaurant that specializes in fancy but not overdone food with a local flair. Our breakfast here was among the better meals we enjoyed during our numerous trips to the lake.

BODIN FISHERIES AND SEAFOOD MARKET

208 Wilson Avenue, Bayfield. www.facebook.com/pages/Bodin-Fisheries/378681247187

Stop by Bodin Fisheries in Bayfield, and you can pick up the catch of the day at the building's little shop while connecting with a still-vital part of the city's history and economy. "I am fourth generation of a fishing family, my great-great-grandfather came from Sweden," says Jeff Bodin. As we talk to Bodin, we're surrounded by an atmosphere that, while lakeside, feels as nautical as anything in Maine or Nova Scotia. The boats, gear, and buildings here are made for catching and processing fish without frills or fuss, the opposite of the plush charter experience we'd enjoyed in Thunder Bay yet distinct also from the romantic small-boat experience we'd had in Knife River.

Bodin buys fish, including smelt, whitefish, and herring, from local fishermen who own their own boats and gear, and then he sells the processed fish to retail, restaurants, hospitals, and other outlets within a hundred miles. In season, the plant processes seven hundred pounds of fish before Thursday, and another seven hundred on Friday.

The fishery skins, splits, scales, bones, filets, smokes, and otherwise gets fish in shape to meet a public demand that, Bodin says, is rising: "There is a lot of buy, eat local push from the Chambers [of Commerce] around," he notes.

Jeff Bodin of Bodin Fisheries in Bayfield.

ACKNOWLEDGMENTS

We are grateful first of all to Pieter Martin at the University of Minnesota Press for reaching out to us and helping us carve this book out of the raw material of curiosity and wanderlust. Cathy Presenger and the City of Thunder Bay took great care of us during our visit and showed us unexpected facets of that rough-cut jewel by the lake. Steve Dahl welcomed us onto his herring skiff and took us out on the lake for one of the finest adventures of our voyage. John Fox clued us in to cudighi and connected us with the remarkable jam-making monks of the Keweenaw Peninsula. Our old friend from Boston, Faye Bowers, earns our thanks for introducing us to Marquette and the Upper Peninsula. And we thank the readers of and contributors to The Heavy Table, who helped give this project both shape and propulsion.

SOURCES

In addition to the publications listed here, the author drew information from numerous periodicals and more than fifty interviews conducted during various trips to places around Lake Superior.

Abrams, Lawrence, and Kathleen Abrams. *Exploring Wisconsin*. New York: Rand McNally and Company, 1983.

Alin, Erika. *Lake Effect: Along Superior's Shores*. Minneapolis: University of Minnesota Press, 2003.

Bogue, Margaret Beatti, and Virginia A. Palmer. *Around the Shores of Lake Superior: A Guide to Historic Sites*. Madison: University of Wisconsin Sea Grant College Program, 1979.

Bray, Matt, and Ernie Epp. *A Vast and Magnificent Land: An Illustrated History of Northern Ontario*. Thunder Bay: Lakehead University, 1984.

Carter, James L., and Ernest H. Rankin. *North to Lake Superior: The Journal of Charles W. Penny, 1840*. Marquette, Mich.: Marquette County Historical Society, 1970.

Chisholm, Barbara, and Andrea Gutsche. *Superior: Under the Shadow of the Gods*. Toronto: Lynx Images, 1998.

Dahl, Stephen. *Knife Island: Circling a Year in a Herring Skiff*. Minneapolis: Nodin Press, 2009.

Dennis, Jerry. *The Living Great Lakes: Searching for the Heart of the Inland Seas*. New York: St. Martin's Press, 2003.

Dierckins, Tony. *Crossing the Canal: An Illustrated History of Duluth's Aerial Bridge*. Duluth: X-Communication, 2008.

Donald, Betsy. "From Kraft to Craft: Innovation and Creativity in Ontario's Food Economy." Working paper series, Ontario in the Creative Age, Martin Prosperity Institute, Rutman School of Management, University of Toronto, 2009. martin prosperity.org.

Dregni, Eric. *Midwest Marvels: Roadside Attractions across Iowa, Minnesota, the Dakotas, and Wisconsin*. Minneapolis: University of Minnesota Press, 2006.

Dunbar, Willis F. (revised by George S. May). *Michigan: A History of the Wolverine State*. Grand Rapids, Mich.: William B. Eerdmans Publishing Company, 1980.

Gianakura, Peter C. *An American Cafe: Reflections from the Grill*. Sault Ste. Marie, Mich.: Peter C. Gianakura, 2009.

Grand Marais Historical Society. *Images of America: Grand Marais*. Chicago: Arcadia Publishing, 2009.

Harris, Walt. *The Chequamegon Country, 1659–1976*. Fayetteville, Ark.: Walter J. Harris, 1976.

Hoverson, Doug. *Land of Amber Waters: The History of Brewing in Minnesota*. Minneapolis: University of Minnesota Press, 2007.

Johnson, Clarence ("Cooper"). *Fitger's: The Brewery and Its People*. Duluth: Fitger's Publishing, 2004.

Lamppa, Marvin G. *Minnesota's Iron Country: Rich Ore, Rich Lives*. Duluth: Lake Superior Port Cities, 2004.

Larson, Paul Clifford. *A Place at the Lake*. Afton, Minn.: Afton Historical Society Press, 1998.

Lydecker, Ryck, and Lawrence J. Sommer, eds. *Duluth: Sketches of the Past*. Duluth: American Revolution Bicentennial Commission, 1976.

McClelland, Ted. *The Third Coast*. Chicago: Chicago Review Press, 2008.

Nordskog, Michael. *The Opposite of Cold: The Northwoods Finnish Sauna Tradition*. Minneapolis: University of Minnesota Press, 2010.

Norton, James, ed. *Minnesota Lunch: From Pasties to Banh Mi*. St. Paul: Minnesota Historical Society Press, 2011.

Oikarinen, Peter. *Island Folk: The People of Isle Royale*. Minneapolis: University of Minnesota Press, 1979.

Ojakangas, Beatrice A. *The Finnish Cookbook*. New York: Crown Publishers, 1989.

Olson, Sigurd F. *Runes of the North*. New York: Alfred Knopf, 1973.

Perich, Shawn. *The North Shore: A Four-Season Guide to Minnesota's Favorite Destination*. Minneapolis: University of Minnesota Press, 2003.

Puotinen, Arthur E. *Finnish Radicals and Religion in Midwestern Mining Towns, 1865–1914*. New York: Arno Press, 1979.

Simonowicz, Nina A. *Nina's North Shore Guide: Big Lake, Big Woods, Big Fun*. 3rd ed. Minneapolis: University of Minnesota Press, 2004.

Wilkes, George. *Angry Trout Notebook: Friends, Recipes, and the Culture of Sustainability*. Grand Marais, Minn.: Northwind Sailing, 2004.

Winckler, Suzanne. *The Smithsonian Guide to Historic America: The Great Lakes States*. New York: Stewart, Tabori, and Chang, 1989.

Wingerd, Mary Lethert. *North Country: The Making of Minnesota*. Minneapolis: University of Minnesota Press, 2010.

The WPA Guide to Minnesota. St. Paul: Minnesota Historical Society Press, 1938.

The WPA Guide to Wisconsin. St. Paul: Minnesota Historical Society Press, 1941.

INDEX

James Norton is the editor of The Heavy Table, a daily online journal of Upper Midwestern food, and a contributor to Csmonitor.com. His previous books include *The Master Cheesemakers of Wisconsin* and *Minnesota Lunch: From Pasties to Banh Mi*. He lives in Minneapolis with his wife, Becca Dilley.

Becca Dilley is a Minneapolis-based wedding, events, and food photographer. She has contributed to numerous books and other editorial projects, and her photographs have appeared in *Saveur*, *Culture: The Word on Cheese*, the Minneapolis/St. Paul *Star Tribune*, and CNN Money.